6-19-74

Manpower and Education in Franco Spain

Manpower and Education in Franco Spain

MORRIS A. HOROWITZ

Archon Books
1974

*A Project of the Inter-University Study
of Human Resources in National
Development*

© 1974 by Morris A. Horowitz
Published 1974 as an Archon Book by
The Shoe String Press, Inc.,
Hamden, Connecticut 06514

Library of Congress Cataloging in Publication Data

Horowitz, Morris Aaron.
   Manpower and education in Franco Spain.

   Includes bibliographical references.
   1. Education—Economic aspects—Spain. 2. Manpower policy—Spain.   I.   Title.

LC67.S7H67   331.1'1   73-8670
ISBN 0-208-01382-2

1810552

To
Jean, Ruth, and Joel

Contents

Foreword   XI
Preface   XIII

I   Introduction   3
     Contents of study
     Background

II   Postwar Political and Economic Development   11
     The immediate post civil war years
     The political scene
     The beginnings of economic planning
     The first and second economic plans

III   The Labor Market Scene: Demand for Labor   25
     General working rules
     Minimum wages and wage rates
     Changes in earnings
     General employment trends
     The demand for labor

IV   Manpower Supply and Targets   44
     The labor force
     The unemployment situation
     Migration and the labor force
     Sources of trained manpower

V   The Processes of Human Capital Formation   61
     The formal educational system
     Primary education
     Secondary education
     Vocational and technical education
     Training programs for adults
     The universities

VI   The System of Higher Education   86
        The university structure
        The university faculties
        The university programs
        Problems of growth
        Student unrest
        Quality of education
        The Autonomous universities
        Changes in the educational system
VII The Processes of Manpower Allocation   109
        Rigidities in the market
        Matching supply and demand
        Efforts at manpower planning
VIII Summary and Conclusions   124
        Summary of the development of manpower in Spain
        Conclusions and policy implications for manpower
            planning
Appendix Tables   133
Notes   155
Index   163

TABLES

 1. Annual Rates of Growth in the Industrial Sector, 1964-1968   20
 2. Economic Plan for 1968-1971   23
 3. Spanish Minimum Wage Scales, 1967   29
 4. Percentage Changes in Prices and Wages, 1960-1968   30
 5. Distribution of Wage and Salary Income, in Constant Pesetas
       of 1963, by Economic Sector   31
 6. Percentage of Workers Receiving Designated Hourly Earnings,
       excluding Family Allowances, 1963-1968   32
 7. Total Employment and Number of Wage and Salary Workers
       by Economic Activity, 1960 and 1968   37
 8. Labor Force by Occupational Groups, 1964 and 1968   39
 9. Number of Persons with a Second Job, According to Weekly
       Hours Worked in Each Activity, 1968   42
10. Distribution of the Labor Force by Sectors, 1960-1968   46
11. Labor Force Trend by Economic Activity, for Selected Years   48
12. Labor Force in Spain by Level of Training, 1965, 1966, 1967 and
       Forecast for 1971   50
13. Trend of Unemployment, 1960-1968   52

14. Comparison of Unemployment Estimates for Various Years 52
15. Labor Force and Unemployment, by Economic Activity,
    1960 and 1968 53
16. Spanish Emigration to Europe (Permanent Residents)
    1959-1967 55
17. Spanish Emigration to Countries Across the Atlantic (Permanent
    Residents) 1959-1968 56
18. Classification of Spanish Population over 15 Years of Age
    According to Schools Attended 63
19. Percentage of Population Attending School, by Age, Spain and
    France, 1966 65
20. Number of Students in the Educational System, by Level of
    Education, 1966-67 and 1967-68 66
21. Students Enrolled in Secondary Education 1965-1966 and
    1967-68 71
22. Student Attrition at Different Levels of the Baccalaureate
    Program, 1951-1967 72
23. Number of Students in Vocational and Technical Education,
    1956-57 to 1966-67 78
24. Enrollments, Graduates and Teachers of Middle Level Technical
    Schools, 1957-58 to 1966-67 81
25. Total Enrollments in Higher Education, 1956-57 to 1967-68 84
26. University Enrollments by University Districts and by Faculty,
    1967-68 90
27. University Enrollments by University Districts, 1955-56 and
    1967-68 97
28. University Enrollments by Faculty, 1955-56 and 1967-68 98
29. Number of Students and Professors at Universities and Techno-
    logical Institutes, 1960-61 through 1968-69 103
30. Drop-Out Rates for Selected Faculties and Branches of Higher
    Education for Official and "Free" Students, 1967-68 103
31. Survival Rates in Various Careers of Higher Education, for
    1965-66, 1966-67 and 1967-68 104
32. Average Annual Manpower Needs and Potential Resources,
    the Educational System, 1967-1971 122

Appendix Tables
III-1. Average Hourly Earnings in Selected Industries, First
       Quarter 1967, 1968, 1969 135
III-2. Employment by Economic Activities, 1966 and Forecast for
       1971 136
III-3. Labor Force by Socioeconomic Groups, 1964-1968 137
III-4. Labor Force by Professional Status and Age Groups, 1968 ... 138
III-5. Labor Force by Professional Status and Hours Worked per
       Week, 1968 139
IV-1. Labor Force by Socioeconomic Groups and Cultural
       Level, 1968 140

IV-2. Percent Distribution of Labor Force by Sex and Age Groups, 1968 141

V-1. Number of Students per 1000 Inhabitants and Percentage Distribution of Enrollments by Level of Education, for Selected Countries 142

V-2. Public Expenditure on Education for Selected Countries, 1968 142

V-3. Preprimary and Primary School Enrollments, and Students per Teacher, 1954-55 through 1967-68 143

V-4. Students in the General Baccalaureate Programs, by Level of Programs, 1958-59 through 1967-68 144

V-5. Students Who Enrolled for Final Exams and Who Passed, at Different Levels of General Baccalaureate Programs, 1958-59 through 1967-68 145

V-6. Enrollment in Technical Baccalaureate Programs by Area of Study, 1959-60 through 1966-67 146

V-7. Number of Students and Professors in State and Non-State Normal Schools, 1957-58 through 1967-68 147

V-8. Enrollments in Industrial Programs of Vocational Education, by Levels of Training, 1960-61 through 1966-67 148

V-9. University Enrollments by Specialty, 1956-57 through 1967-68 149

V-10. Number of University Students Who Completed their Studies, by Specialty, 1956-57 through 1967-68 150

V-11. Enrollments in Engineering Institutes, by Specialty, 1956-57 through 1967-68 151

V-12. Number of Students of Engineering Institutes Who Completed their Studies, by Specialty, 1956-57 through 1967-68 152

VI-1. "Free" Students as a Percentage of Total Enrollments, by Faculty, for Selected Years 153

FOREWORD

This book is an important contribution to the growing literature in English on manpower policies and education in particular countries. The development of trained and competent manpower resources is an essential part of the economic development and modernization process of every nation. Comparatively little has been known about this relationship in Spain, a nation which for reasons the author presents in detail has only lately undertaken to establish goals of rapid economic growth and acceptance in the European common market system.

The author is particularly well-qualified to undertake a field study in Spain. He is an established scholar of manpower policies and their relation to educational systems in the U.S. and abroad. Under the auspices of the Ford Foundation, he spent a year in Argentina during 1961-62, as a consultant to the Center for Economic Research of the Instituto Torcuato Di Tella in a study of high-level manpower in Argentina. Subsequently, he contributed the lead essay, "High-Level Manpower in the Economic Development of Argentina," to the volume, *Manpower and Education: Country studies in Economic Development,* edited by Professor Frederick Harbison of Princeton University and myself, published in 1965. This was one of the projects sponsored by the Inter-University Study of Labor Problems in Economic Development (now known as the Inter-University Study of Human Resources in National Development).

When Professor Horowitz was given a leave of absence by his University, the Inter-University Board was happy to contribute funds to making it possible for him to spend an entire year in Spain during 1969-70. Only one earlier study, by the Mediterranean Regional Project of the Organization for Economic Cooperation and Development (OECD), had been made in Spain prior to Horowitz's study, and that was based largely on 1960 data confined to the formal educational system. Professor Horowitz has looked at the process of manpower development more broadly, in the context of recent economic development efforts. In addition to the formal education system, which is being overhauled for the first time in many years, he has looked at vocational and technical education, training programs for adults, and on-the-job training.

The lack of systematic manpower planning for future needs is apparent in the fact that the Planning Commission has largely ignored it, leaving to the Education Ministry and other groups what short-term planning there is in efforts to meet skilled labor and technical manpower shortages. A notable exception to this generalization appears to be the training of people to staff the expanding tourist facilities in Spain, an important source of foreign exchange for industrial development.

Students and scholars in the fields of educational development, manpower planning, manpower policies, and economic development policies will find this book a rich source of new data and insights into the interrelationships of these fields. Even the topic of student unrest, the subject of another Inter-University Study-financed volume,[1] is discussed in the chapter on higher education, though Spain is still (at this writing) a dictatorship and universities are tightly controlled.

CHARLES A. MYERS

Massachusetts Institute of Technology

[1] E. Wight Bakke and Mary S. Bakke, *Campus Challenge: Student Activism in Perspective* (Hamden, Connecticut: Archon Books, 1971).

Preface

Manpower and education as critical factors in the growth and development of nations began to appear in the literature of economics with some regularity only during the past fifteen or so years. However, it was not until 1964, when Frederick Harbison and Charles A. Myers published their landmark book, *Education, Manpower, and Economic Growth*, that these factors became widely accepted as major explanations of economic growth. This book revolutionized the literature on development by focusing on human resources, and by presenting a generalized concept of human resource development with appropriate policies and strategies that could be used by economic planners. The following year Harbison and Myers edited a volume, *Manpower and Education*, which contained case studies of manpower and education in eleven less developed countries. These two volumes generated the interest that has resulted in a number of studies of the effects of human resources development on the growth of developing nations.

The present study of manpower and education in Franco Spain follows the general pattern set by these previous volumes. Obviously, however, the environmental factors in a nation such as Franco Spain differ from those of other nations, and as a result the framework of the present study has some unique characteristics. The long-enduring authoritarian government has had its impact on all facets of life in Spain, and on the pace and paths of economic growth.

The general scope of the study is the development of manpower and education in Spain and their effects on the economic growth of the nation. The principal factors involved are the educational systems and the size and composition of the labor force. Impinging on these factors in order to manipulate, regulate, and control them are various institutions such as government agencies, the church, the "sindicatos," private organizations, as well as economic, political, social, and cultural factors. The study is concerned with the role these factors have played in manpower and education development, and what impact, if any, manpower and education had on the económic growth of the country.

A principal theme of the study is how an authoritarian society, such as Franco Spain, manages and manipulates its manpower and educational planning in an effort to speed the process of economic growth and development. Various forces are at work, often with conflicting goals and aims. While the Franco government has the power to issue decrees and orders affecting the labor market, the educational systems, and the labor force, implementing such decrees and orders is considerably more difficult. Bureaucratic and political groups within the government and outside it are vying for power or a more favorable government position, and the frequent result is a stand-off in the implementation of a government policy. An informal system of checks and balances has developed over the years effectively limiting the authoritarian power of the Franco government. The result is that Spain has had no greater success in planning and directing its human resources with authoritarian power than have nations such as the United States.

Another major theme is the rapid growth in recent years of the training and educational systems, and the systems' failure in supplying sufficient persons with the necessary skills, training, and education to meet the needs of the growing economy. Spain has a long tradition of training and education, and many of its institutions go back for centuries. However, these systems have built up bureaucracies, encrusted with traditions and with vested interests in maintaining the status quo. Recent efforts to change the systems have had minimal results. The systems therefore offer basically the same scope of programs and study offered over thirty years ago. With only slight variations the training and educational institutions offer study programs to the Spanish youths for the same trades and professions offered to the youths' parents. In addition, social and cultural values place prestige on certain occupations and professions, which influences a substantial proportion of youths to study for these occupations and professions although they already are significantly overcrowded.

A third important theme is the view of substantial numbers of bureaucrats, professionals, and government technicians that planned human resources development is not an important factor in the economic growth of Spain. For some who maintain this view the rationale is that there is a shortage of all kinds of manpower, and that at the present stage of Spain's development the economy needs any and every type of manpower. For others, the rationale is more political. These persons refuse to recognize the importance of manpower because of the political overtones involved in any effort to plan human resource development.

This study is not a history of manpower and education in Spain, although some history is presented where it is considered relevant to an understanding of the themes of the study. Chapter II, for example, describes in broad strokes the political and economic setting of modern Spain, in order to set the scene for the analysis of the demand and supply of labor and of the processes of human capital formation. Chapter III analyzes the operation of the labor market and its demand for labor, and chapter IV describes the formation of manpower supply and the supply targets. Chapter V and VI describe and analyze the processes of human capital formation, with special emphasis on vocational training and on the system of higher education. Chapter VII analyzes the processes of manpower allocation in labor markets of the nation, describing the market forces as well as the efforts at manpower planning. The final chapter contains a summary of the development of manpower in Spain, and conclusions and policy implications for manpower planning.

The idea for this study came to me in the fall of 1968, when I began reading a number of reports on the economic and social planning in Spain. At that time relatively little was being published in English on what was happening in this rapidly growing economy. I developed a working outline, and from September, 1969, through August, 1970, while on sabbatical leave from my professorship in economics at Northeastern University, I did the field research in Spain. When I returned to the United States, I still had considerable material to assimilate, and additional data and reports continued to be sent me from my contacts in Spain. The process of collecting additional data is a continuous one, but at some point the value of more current material is negligible. The effective cut-off point of this study is the end of 1971.

In my field work in Spain I interviewed and held informal conferences with numerous persons, and just "talked" with many others. They ranged from high government officials to taxi drivers, from university professors to waiters. I am pleased to state that all were friendly and made some effort to be of assistance to me in my research. A number spent considerable time with me aiding me in my search for ideas, information and materials. I thus became indebted to numerous persons—more than can be legitimately listed in a preface, and I take this opportunity to thank them all. Some debts, however, are larger than others, and to my largest creditors, without whom this study could not have been completed, I must make public acknowledgements.

To the following persons in Spain I owe a special thanks for the extra time and effort they spent in helping me in numerous ways in my research:

José Ramón Lasuén, Dean of Facultad de Ciencias Económicas, Autonomous University, Madrid; Alejandro Lorca, Professor of Economics, University of Valencia; Amando de Miguel, Professor of Sociology, Autonomous University, Barcelona; António Lago Carballo,

Professor of History, University of Madrid; José María Esteban Vargas, Economist, Ministry of Labor, Madrid; Aristóbulo de Juan, Secretary General, Banco Popular Español; António Luna Barrales, Director General, Sociedad de Investigación Económica; and Efrén Borrajo Dacruz, Director General de Promoción Social, Ministry of Labor.

My greatest indebtedness is to Charles A. Myers, Professor of Industrial Relations, Massachusetts Institute of Technology. It was with him that I discussed the original research idea, and he made many helpful suggestions. Professor Myers, as a member of the Coordinating Board of the Inter-University Study of Human Resources in National Development, presented my research project to the Coordinating Board and it agreed to help finance my research. I thus owe a special thanks to the other board members, Clark Kerr of University of California at Berkeley, John T. Dunlop of Harvard University, and Frederick Harbison of Princeton University, for this support of my research. Professor Myers also critically reviewed the entire manuscript and gave me many useful comments.

I wish to extend a special thanks to my secretary, Miss Rosalie N. Parechanian, for the arduous chore she undertook of deciphering my handwriting and typing the manuscript a number of times. A public thanks is also due to Mrs. Sylvia R. Goldberg, Miss Domenica E. Amato, and Miss Dianne Genovese for assisting in the typing of tables and other materials.

Needless to say, none of the many people who assisted me in this study is responsible for any of its shortcomings. I bear sole responsibility for the views and judgments presented in this study and also for all the errors.

MORRIS A. HOROWITZ

Northeastern University
Boston

Manpower and Education in Franco Spain

I

INTRODUCTION

As a result of internal and external factors, Spain has changed significantly during the decades of the 1950s and 1960s. The greatest observable changes have been in the economic sphere, but some social and political changes have also taken place. Undoubtedly these changes are not only affected by outside phenomena but they also affect each other. Which are causes and which effects are not readily ascertainable. In Spain, more so than in an open society, it becomes almost impossible to disentangle the web of events that affect political, social, and economic changes, and that become such changes. This study is not the vehicle to analyze these fa tors in depth.

One can examine and analyze Spain and its recent changes from many viewpoints, and each is likely to prove interesting and informative. However, the author has selected a rather narrow focus—that of the manpower in Spain. Basically, this study is concerned with the institutions and factors that have affected human resource development, and with the role manpower has played in the economic changes of the country. The importance of social and political factors in human resource development are also examined.

The significance of human resource development has long been recognized by economists, going back as far as Adam Smith. As a concomitant of economic development, human resource development is the process of increasing the knowledge, skills, and the capacities of all the people in a society.[1] Our concern is thus with the various ways persons are developed, such as, for example, education and training, and the impact of these on the modernization of a nation. A study of manpower in Spain may provide some insights into the development process of that country, and perhaps of other countries as well.

Clearly, in order to understand the role of manpower in any economy, one must examine how the labor markets function and how various economic, political, and social factors affect the labor markets. Inherent in the functioning of labor markets is the demand for and the supply of different types and levels of manpower. The composition of this labor demand is based on the technology used and the levels of economic activity. The composition of the labor supply is determined by a number of factors, an important one of which is education and training.

Contents of Study

Different political and economic settings unquestionably establish some constraints on the functioning of labor markets, and these settings must therefore be described to set the scene for our study of human resource development. Franco's dictatorship of Spain has had a strong influence on all aspects of the country. Chapter II attempts to describe in broad strokes the political and economic setting of modern Spain. Franco's Spain is not monolithic; within the functioning political groups are the Falangists on the right and the radical Catholic groups on the left, with clandestine left-wing groups surfacing on various occasions. Until relatively recently Franco managed to keep his government well balanced among the various groups that supported him; heads of ministries changed and minor shifts in power occurred, but the overall composition of the administration remained unchanged. In the mid-1950s he opened his government to a new group, Opus Dei, an activist Roman Catholic lay organization which espoused a liberal economic policy. In 1969 Opus Dei was given control of the government, with the apparent policy of modernizing Spain and changing it sufficiently to bring it into the Common Market. As a result of recent economic policies Spain has attained a relatively high level of industrial growth. A rapidly rising level of national income has placed Spain within the range generally considered semi-developed. The urban middle class has grown rapidly and is now the owners of automobiles, televisions, hi-fi's, and many of the home electrical appliances that represent an affluent society.

Chapter II also points up the early attempts of the Franco regime at self-sufficiency, and its failures. In the late 1950s Spain was opened to foreign investment and trade and, at the recommendation of the World Bank, an economic stabilization program was adopted. The apparent success of the stabilization policies gave the government encouragement for further planning. A planning commission was established and the first economic plan for the years 1964-1967 was developed. Rapid economic growth continued and a second plan for the period 1968-1971 was produced. Within this political, social, and economic framework there evolved the policies and institutions relating to manpower and education in Spain.

Chapter III examines and analyzes the institutions and factors affecting the functioning of labor markets in Spain. The chapter focuses on the demand side of the market, and attempts to differentiate between the private and the public sectors. General working rules are described, and their impact on the functioning of labor markets is analyzed. Wage rates and earnings are examined to determine their relations with the demand for labor. Employment trends for various breakdowns of occupations and industries are presented and analyzed. These various demand factors are placed within the context of Franco's Spain, with its authoritarian powers and its indicative economic planning.

Chapter IV focuses on the supply of Spain's manpower, in the context of the manpower targets indicated by the country's economic plans. Data on the labor force are presented, and its composition is analyzed in terms of industry, occupation, and socioeconomic level. The growth of the labor supply is traced and the changing structure analyzed. The importance of emigration as a release from the pressures of unemployment is studied. Permanent emigration has been a relatively constant but minor factor in Spain's unemployment situation, but during the past decade temporary migration to Western European countries has had a significant cumulative effect on Spain's manpower picture. Surprisingly, however, the Spanish returnees with a few years of industrial work experience generally did not find work in Spain which made use of their new skills.

In order to comprehend the basic source of the labor supply, chapter V describes and analyzes the various processes of human capital formation in Spain. An effort is made to show how the formal educational system, despite its broad base and compulsory nature, discriminates against lower-income families. Very recent changes in the laws pertaining to the educational system call for widening educational opportunities, but basic changes are likely to be slow in coming. A significant part of secondary education is provided in private schools, and, in general, the private education is superior to the public. Vocational and technical education is provided free in the public system, but relatively little has been done to determine which skills are needed in the market place. An unknown amount of on-the-job training is done by private firms. Because of the significant shifts in the labor force in recent years from the agricultural to the industrial sector of the economy, various training programs for adults have been started. Some of these have been rather effective, while others have not been. At the professional level the universities have increased enrollments substantially in the past ten years, but the growth has principally been in the traditional professions, and not in those where the market needs are growing more rapidly.

Because of the importance of high-level manpower to the rapid industrialization of Spain, all of chapter VI is devoted to the nation's system of higher education. The university structure is described in some detail, and the rigidities of the system of higher education are analyzed. Despite the controls in the nation, student unrest hit Spain as it hit other nations around the world. Student strikes and protests occurred for a wide range of reasons, from political to the quality of university education. Despite efforts by the government to quash the protests and the protest groups, the students have continued to apply pressures to gain their ends. Various changes (mostly improvements) have been made in the universities, due partly, perhaps, to the pressures of students. New universities with much greater flexibility in programs have been created by the government.

Chapter VII discusses the processes of manpower allocation, and why the supply of and demand for labor in the labor markets do not mesh. Numerous rigidities, both legal and institutional, hinder the operations of the marketplace, and the matching of supply and demand in any labor market is no more than chance. The planning commission has made no effort at detailed manpower planning in the public or the private sector of the economy. However, in peripheral government agencies some minor efforts are being made to develop a program for projecting detailed manpower requirements and manpower supply.

Chapter VIII summarizes the basic findings and presents the conclusions. The State has had and continues to have the dominant role in the market, but over the past decade the private enterprise has been permitted to assume a growing amount of flexibility and economic freedom. A shift in the power in government to Opus Dei has meant greater emphasis on world markets, economic growth and development, the private enterprise and the free market mechanism. Opus Dei in power has meant more technocrats in the government, and economic planning has been focused principally on finance and investment. The modernization of some industries has placed a premium on skilled workers and technicians; in some industries, however, the shortage of such skilled workers and technicians has resulted in the failure to invest in more sophisticated machinery and equipment, the operation of which required these workers. Because needed manpower had not been in short supply in the past, no effort has been made by the planning commission to engage in manpower planning. Thus, while various factors have motivated firms to expand and modernize, the institutions that educate and train manpower have changed very little. Manpower is being developed with little or no relationship to the requirements of the labor market. At this point productivity is lower than it need be, and unemployment pressures are being released by short-term emigration. If this process continues, unemployment could rise substantially while low productivity could cause a serious deterioration in Spain's trade. It is becoming more critical that Spain take the necessary steps to plan the development of its manpower to meet the needs of the market.

Background

Franco's Spain, and all that it connotes, undoubtedly has been the major factor in molding the education and training institutions as well as the labor market institutions. Generalissimo Francisco Franco has been dictator of Spain for over thirty years, and over this period the country has changed very significantly. The original authoritarian aspects of the government have loosened markedly, and there is considerably greater participation by institutions and organizations in the country's governance than before. There is greater acceptability of limited protest against the government and its policies, although the state can be exceedingly harsh where protest exceeds some invisible limits. There is a feeling of greater political freedom, but there is also the knowledge that on major issues relating to the politics of Spain the decisions are made by Franco and his coterie of advisors.

On the economic side, the country has moved from a policy of autarky and self-sufficiency to one of limited free enterprise. Foreign investment is being encouraged and market forces are being given greater freedom. Wages and prices are still being regulated, but with greater flexibility, and many other controls are gradually being loosened. While inflation is still a problem, the general buoyancy of the economy has resulted in great optimism among the population.

Within this political and economic setting is a population of about 33.3 million people in a geographic area with a density rate of 65 persons per square kilometer. The annual growth rate of the Spanish population has been about one percent, which is low in comparison with the growth in most less developed or semi-developed countries around the world. Unlike almost all other Roman Catholic countries, Spain's crude birthrate is relatively low, with 20.1 live births per 1,000 persons, compared with 21.5 in Ireland, 22.3 in Argentina, 24.5 in Puerto Rico, and 30.9 in Chile. Spain's crude death rate was 9.2 per thousand, and its infant mortality rate was 30.0 per thousand.[2]

One possible explanation of the rather low birthrate in Spain is that the average Spaniard does not marry young. The following statistics for a number of countries in 1965 show the proportion of marriages in which the men and the women are under 25 years of age.[3]

COUNTRY	MEN	WOMEN	TOTAL
Spain	23.3%	57.9%	40.6%
France	52.4	72.3	62.5
Sweden	48.5	71.7	60.1
Italy	27.4	63.8	45.6
Greece	21.2	56.5	38.9
Portugal	40.1	64.5	52.3
Ireland	32.6	55.3	43.9

Only 23 percent of the men getting married were under 25 years of age, compared to 52 percent in France and 48 percent in Switzerland. The delay in marriage apparently is an effective form of birth control. In addition, a more than average number of women in Spain remained unmarried, again having an impact on the birth rate. The overall popula tion growth in Spain is low, and the average household size is relatively small with 4.3 persons. The average size of the household unit ranged from 3.7 persons for families with very low income to 4.9 for very high income families.[4]

The industrial development of Spain has not been uniform throughout the country, and as a result there is a regular, rather large movement of persons from the less developed provinces to the industrial centers, and from small towns and rural communities to the larger cities.[5] Economic pressures of unemployment, underemployment, and low income have resulted in considerable emigration to other countries. While the movement to the Western Hemisphere has not been large, the migration to other European countries has been quite significant. According to one estimate approximately 1.9 million Spaniards have migrated to other European countries over the eight-year period 1960-1967, of whom about 900,000 were seasonal migrants.[6] The one million so-called permanent migrants during this eight-year period represent close to 8 percent of the country's labor force.

An estimated 12.6 million persons were in the labor force, which represented about 38 percent of Spain's 33 million population. In 1969 about 30 percent of the labor force was in the agricultural sector, a significant decline from the 41 percent in 1960.[7] Illiteracy in the labor force in 1969 was only 4 percent, but it was 6 percent in the total population, and 8 percent in the population over 14 years of age. And as one would expect, the largest percentage of illiteracy was found among agricultural and personal service workers.[8]

By 1969 the GNP per capita in Spain had reached $825, a gain of about 56 percent in five years, and a level well within the range generally considered semideveloped. Spain shows a degree of inequality in the distribution of income somewhat larger than that of the developed European countries but significantly less than that of underdeveloped countries. The wealthiest 5 percent of Spaniards received between 17 and 19 percent of total income, but there has been a slow trend toward a distribution of income with less inequality.[9] By 1970 the middle class represented between 45 and 49 percent of Spanish society.[10]

In the early 1960s a number of studies asserted that there were obstacles to development in the Spanish economy or serious flaws in the industrial structure.[11] For the International Bank, one of the principal problems facing the Spanish economy was that in many industries firms were too small to operate efficiently, a situation partly attributable to the tradition of small-scale family enterprise, which has been maintained longer in Spain than in most other European countries. And an accompanying problem is that of obsolete or inefficient equipment, which has handicapped Spanish industry through low productivity and poor quality of consumer goods and intermediate products.[12] The Banco de Bilbao saw the same problems and a number of others, such as the inequality of income distribution, the low proportion of the population in the labor force, and the high proportion of the labor force in agriculture.[13]

Both these reports indicated that Spain's most important development assets were an abundant supply of industrious and easily trained manpower, an able managerial class, and an established financial community. Apparently these assets were sufficiently important to offset the liabilities of the economic system. By the end of the decade of the 1960s, Spain had made considerable progress in its economic advancement. Nevertheless a 1968 study of Spain by the OECD cited the continued existence of many industries with firms that were too small to function efficiently and of farms either too small or too large for optimum operations.[14]

While describing itself as neither a capitalist nor a socialist economy, Spain operates a limited free-enterprise system, with the government an active participant in many economic sectors through the National Institute of Industry (INI), a government-owned organization created in 1941. INI's function is to promote and finance new or existing industries, and it has the authority to obtain the total or partial expropriation of any industrial or mining enterprise, or to compel such an enterprise to enlarge its capital so that the Institute may hold a majority participation. Despite this power, no private enterprises have been nationalized since the INI was established.[15] In 1969, INI participated directly in 71 firms, most of which are completely state-owned, and the total assets amounted to about $1.7 billion. The government participation amounted to over 50 percent in industries such as aluminum, cellulose, ships, automobiles, and buses; and over a 30 percent participation in electric power, mining, petroleum refining, fertilizer, and air transportation. INI's participation in the steel industry was 26 percent.[16]

Registered unemployment in Spain has been consistently low, at or below 2 percent, but it has been generally recognized that these official statistics understate the problem significantly. A recent survey reports unemployment in Madrid in 1969 at about 6 percent, and unemployment in other parts of Spain would be at least as high. The same report notes that in Madrid about 20 percent of the wage and salary workers hold two or more jobs.[17]

The standard of living, especially in the urban areas, has risen substantially in recent years. Housing, however, has been a long-run difficult problem. Statistics show that in 1967 there was a shortage of some 1.7 million housing units, at a time when about 20 percent of existing housing was over 100 years old; and it was estimated that in 1976 the deficit will still be in excess of one million, about the same deficit that existed in 1961.[18]

In 1969, a survey showed that 99 percent of the households had electricity, 80 percent had running water, 62 percent had bath or shower, and 39 percent had a telephone. The same report indicated that 86 percent had a radio, 63 percent a refrigerator, 62 percent television, 43 percent a washing machine, 27 percent an automobile, and 25 percent a phonograph.[19] Well over half the population was covered by the full scope of the social security system, which provides subsidies for marriages, births and deaths, unemployment compensation equal to 55 percent of base pay, disability benefits, limited credit facilities, and a wide range of free medical care.[20] Although still considerably behind the other nations of Western Europe, there seems little doubt that by the end of the decade of the 1960's Spain was rapidly becoming a consumer-oriented country.

This brief description of the social milieu may contribute to an understanding of the operation of labor markets in Spain. While the forces of demand for manpower are not readily affected, the cultural factor of "enchufe,"[21] or connection, does have a bearing in certain industries and occupations on who gets the better, or the available, jobs. The forces of supply of manpower are more directly affected through such factors as population changes and movements, pressures to participate in the labor force, the growing availability of vocational training and education, and the demonstration effects of high incomes and consumer products. The institutional aspects of the labor market are affected not only by the social milieu, but also by various political and economic factors. These will be discussed in the following chapter.

II

POSTWAR POLITICAL
AND ECONOMIC DEVELOPMENT

There is little doubt but that Spain's postwar political and economic development has had a substantial impact upon all aspects of living, including those of manpower and education. The institutional framework of the labor market and the functioning of this market have changed substantially over time as a result of the changing political and economic framework of the country. In order to understand the problems of manpower and education in Spain it is necessary to have a feel of the political and economic environment in which the problems of the various labor markets arise.

While many Western European countries have experienced postwar growth and development, the political and economic situation of Spain is significantly different from that of other countries. In many ways, Spain is unique in Western Europe, and knowledge of other nations may be of little help in understanding the Spanish scene. It therefore becomes important to present a short account of the postwar political and economic changes in Spain and brief description of the current scene.

The Immediate Post Civil War Years

Generalissimo Francisco Franco's dictatorship of Spain has continued from the Spanish Civil War of 1936-1939 for more than thirty years—longer than any other living ruler of a European nation.

Spain became politically and economically isolated in the postwar period, owing largely to the reaction of most nations to the civil war and to Spain's subsequent stand during World War II. As a result, a concerted effort was made to develop a self-sufficient nation. The economy was reorganized into a system of national vertical syndicates for each major field of economic activity, similar to the corporate state of Mussolini's Italy, and in each syndicate employers and workers are organized functionally by major branches of production.

Reminiscent of the medieval system of guilds, its philosophical basis rested on Roman Catholic social theory. The government became directly involved in the nation's economic activities in 1941 with the creation of the National Industrial Institute (INI), a major official instrument for the promotion of industry in fields related to national defense and economic self-sufficiency.[1]

Poor harvests in 1939, 1940, and 1941 resulted in real starvation in Spain, and it was not until 1951 that food supplies returned to pre-1936 levels.[2] The immediate postwar years were critical, and the government was compelled to impose a strict and extensive system of controls and to intervene in many aspects of economic life. Prices, foreign trade and payments, investment, employment, and allocation of raw materials were among the items subjected to regulation. And since Spain could not count on obtaining various needed products from abroad, the government tried to meet the emergency by encouraging the exploitation of native resources not previously regarded as economical.[3]

Price and wage controls were used extensively in the early postwar years in an effort to stabilize the economy, but the level of control was not totally pervasive. Direct price controls were confined to such basic essentials as coal, electricity, gas, minerals, metals, and building materials.[4] In addition to direct controls, the government introduced some structural changes in the economy in an effort to alleviate both the economic and the political environment. In 1939, for example, the government placed a limit of 25 percent on the portion of foreign capital that could be invested in national industries, although in special cases a higher percentage was allowable.[5] New industry was generated by INI in a variety of ways. Financed principally by grants from the national government (almost entirely based on government-created credits, with considerable short-run inflationary effects) INI either created firms outright or participated with private capital in the new enterprise or the expansion of existing plants.[6]

Whether Spain's policy of economic autarky was principally a result of economic necessity or of political choice is a moot point. There is considerable evidence, however, that the postwar ostracism of Spain did push her into a policy of economic nationalism. The fairly widespread boycott of trade with Spain resulted in drastic cuts in both exports and imports. One study[7] indicates the following decline in Spain's trade:

	INDEX OF EXPORT VOLUME	INDEX OF IMPORT VOLUME
1935	100	100
1941	46	45
1945	68	47
1948	73	70
1950	98	64

When World War II ended Spain did not participate in the Marshall Plan. Other Western European countries sought multilateral solutions to their problems, but the Spanish government persevered with its plans which tended to accentuate the isolation of the economy.[8]

The growth of the Spanish economy from 1940 to 1950 was very low, and accompanied by severe inflation. According to the World Bank, "By 1950 it is doubtful whether national income—and *a fortiari* income per head—had recovered even to the depressed level of 1935."[9] While prewar data are scarce, various sources confirm the fact that over the decade of the 1940s the Spanish economy showed very little advancement. According to an ILO report, until 1950 the Spanish economic policy did not follow a defined plan, and economic growth was insignificant while income per inhabitant did not increase.[10] Statistics published by the Bank of Bilbao showed that real per capita national income in 1963 pesetas was 30, 675 in 1940 and 30,494 in 1950.[11]

A marked change in the economic situation began taking place in 1951, largely due to a loan obtained from the United States. National income in 1951 exceeded that of 1935, and income per capita rose appreciably. The western boycott on trade with Spain and on assistance to Spain more-or-less ended with the 1953 Pact of Madrid, which consisted of three interrelated agreements between the United States and Spain: a Defense Agreement, specifically concerned with bases; a Mutual Defense Assistance Agreement, providing American loan, equipment and training facilities for Spanish armed forces; and an Economic Aid Agreement. These marked a turning point in Spain's international isolation and her acceptance as a partner of the United States.[12] After years of isolation and economic hardship, Spain finally began an opening to the world and a period of growth. A combination of factors such as economic aid, internal growth, and the beginning of tourist traffic had its impact in generating a period of prosperity. And in December 1954 Spain obtained entry into the United Nations, thus terminating the final strings of isolation.

The tragedy of the war years and the immediate postwar years, along with the economic deprivation during this period, had their impact upon the adult population of the 1960s. There is considerable evidence that for the vast majority of the population and of political and economic groups, political compromise would be preferred to political anarchy or violence. According to one source:

> . . . it must be constantly borne in mind to what an extent the Civil War still haunts the national memory after more than thirty years. It does so, however, in a manner entirely different from that in which it still haunts the international stage. Whereas abroad, memories of the Spanish Civil War still perpetuate ideological conflict, within Spain they are a grim reminder of the dangers of such a conflict. They have engendered a widespread determination

that this shall not come to pass again, and that the national future must be found by a process of mutual adjustment.[13]

In interviews with numerous Spaniards covering the political spectrum from left to right, the author got similar responses: the Spanish population in general would not accept fighting in the streets again. Regardless of political leanings and attitudes toward Franço's dictatorship, most Spaniards commented favorably on Franco as a leader because of his ability to keep Spain at peace for over thirty years. This does not mean that under certain conditions groups from the left, the right, or the military might not resort to force, but such force is likely to gain little popular support.

The Political Scene
Franco's original power stemmed from his position in the military, and his principal support was from the military. However, it was the Falange, the right-wing political organization with a mass popular support, that spearheaded the war to overthrow the republican government. The Falangists accepted Franco as leader, and he recognized the Falange as the only legal political party in the nation.[14] The Catholic Church was a third significant political power that had favored the overthrow of the republican government, and Franco also accepted this group into his administration. Thus, Franco ruled the nation with a broad coalition government, composed principally of his friends from the military, the Falangists, and conservative Christian Democrats.

Through the years Franco managed to keep his government well balanced among the various groups that supported him. Heads of ministries changed and minor shifts in power occurred, but the overall composition of the administration remained unchanged. In the mid-1950s Franco first agreed to liberalize the economy, but on the condition that the political system remain untouched. It was then that he opened his government to a new group, Opus Dei, an activist Roman Catholic lay organization whose avowed purpose was to bring religious practice into its members' daily life, especially into their work.[15] Apparently, this was a group that espoused a liberal economic policy in line with what Franco saw as necessary for Spain at that time, and of the various political forces Franco considered Opus Dei as the only one with leadership and foresight to move the country forward through economic development.

One of the first actions taken by the new Opus Dei ministers was to create a new structure at the cabinet level to promote the coordination of economic policy making. A new policy of monetary controls was instituted, forcing the bank rate up, and to reduce the budget deficit the government carried out a tax reform of increasing direct taxes and reducing indirect taxes.[16] Consultations were also held with the Organization for European Economic Cooperation (which subsequently became the Organization for Economic Cooperation and Development), the World Bank, and the International Monetary Fund. Spain became a member of IMF and the World Bank in 1958 and the OEEC in 1959.

Known as technocrats, Opus Dei members entered the government in increasing numbers and successfully influenced policies that opened the country to free enterprise and to foreign investment, trade, and tourism. At the same time, Opus Dei members gained control of or influence over a large part of the country's banking, insurance, construction, and communications industries. They contend that their rise to top positions in politics, banking, business, education, and publishing is the result of individual, not group efforts. Whether Opus Dei is a politically cohesive group is debatable, and the nature, purpose and scope of the organization has become Spain's prime political topic.[17] However, there is a rebel faction of Opus Dei which publishes a daily afternoon paper, *Madrid*. This paper has attacked the policies of the government on various occasions and in 1968, under its censorship policies, the government closed down the paper for four months.

Despite its lack of a large popular base, Opus Dei did gain in political power. By 1960 its members were well represented in Franco's cabinet, and they controlled the economic planning organization of the government. These political gains were made at the expense of the Falangists, who nevertheless continued to have the largest representation in the government as well as the largest political base among the population. The strength of its popular support was based on its control over the "sindicatos," or syndicates, the Spanish equivalent of trade unions.[18]

With the participation in the government of various groups, Francisco Franco with great political adroitness managed to balance them off so that no one faction could claim a special advantageous position. Although Spain has some of the trappings of public participation in government, Spain is a kingdom, by law since 1947, but no king has been placed on the throne. Franco, a Chief of State for life, Commander in Chief of the Armed Forces, Prime Minister, and head of the National Movement, exercises absolute power. Although the Law of Succession calls for selection of a successor by the Council of the Regency, it also permits Franco to appoint his successor. In July 1969 Franco appointed Prince Juan Carlos, the son of the pretender, Don Juan, as his eventual successor. The cabinet of eighteen ministers acts as the principal advisory body to the General. The legislative body, the Cortes, has over 500 members, most of whom are appointed by Franco or are members by virtue of their position, e.g., mayors. The sindicatos also elect representatives, and as of 1966 heads of families and married women were given the right to elect 108 members, two from each province. Despite its appearance, the Cortes does not initiate legislation, but ratifies bills formulated by the cabinet.

Franco's hand in the governance of Spain remains throughout all parts of the political system. Not only does he directly or indirectly appoint a majority of persons in the Cortes, he also nominates the President of the Cortes and appoints (and dismisses) all cabinet ministers. He also appoints provincial governors, all heads of sindicatos, all armed forces commanders, and even (by virtue of the 1953 concordat with the Pope) all bishops.[19] There is little doubt that Spain has an authoritarian government, in which all major or important decisions and policies are made by General Franco.

One area of change is that of labor-management relations. Prior to 1958 conditions of employment in the various branches of economic activity were determined through labor regulations. In 1958 the Trade Union Collective Agreements Act was promulgated, legalizing the practice of collective bargaining. Collective agreements are thus becoming the basic instrument for determining conditions of employment, although the agreements do need the government's approval to take effect. Disputes arising out of collective bargaining are settled either by labor administration authorities or by the labor courts, and there has been a notable increase in such settlement of disputes made by authorities.[20]

In October 1969 a basic change took place in the government. For many years the government under Franco was a combination of forces, which the Generalissimo balanced with great skill. For reasons that point to old age and interest in retirement, Franco reshuffled his cabinet and gave Opus Dei virtually complete control of the government. The Opus Dei leader in the government is Laureano López Rodó, the Minister of Planning. Two other Ministers are members of Opus Dei, and another is an auxiliary member. Of the fifteen other Ministers, all but six are close associates of Mr. López Rodó, or his ally Vice President Luis Carrero Blanco. The reaction of this change in government was strong, especially by the Falange and the conservative Christian Democrats, both of which lost considerable power.[21]

Opposition to the government became more open, and what was most troublesome was that much of the opposition came from elements that still considered themselves as segments of the regime. Groups centered around the Falange began working openly to discredit and bring down the new government, and their main element was a $200 million scandal involving a textile machinery company, Matessa, which used government credit to finance partly imaginary exports. Two former ministers and the former head of the Bank of Spain, all of them Opus Dei members, have been indicted. Other counts of criticism against the government included the shaky economic situation, the conduct of the negotiations with the United States over military bases and other foreign policy questions, and restrictions on freedom.[22]

In an effort to divert some of the opposition, the government took a step toward permitting political action in Spain for the first time since the Civil War, but it stopped far short of permitting parties or organized dissent. The law would allow any Spaniard aged eighteen or over to join or form "political associations," but it contained numerous prohibitions on political activities and many detailed and strict rules on operation and organization of political groups. It was not expected to have any immediate practical effect, but it indicated a slow softening of the rules Franco had enforced since 1939.[23]

On various issues the Falangists and the conservative Christian Democrats have joined with the traditional opposition, who were always on the outside, to work against the new cabinet. In the press, in the middle echelons of the ministries, and in the Parliament the government has found itself under constant attack by people whose records in the regime make them immune from the kind of pressure that can be used on the traditional opposition. And two of the leading newspapers, which in the past supported the government, have also begun to criticize openly some of the actions and policies of the new government.[24] On June 25, 1970, Emilio Romero Goméz, member of the parliament, editor of the newspaper *Pueblo* and director of the Official School of Journalism gave a speech on the topic "The Political Forces of Spain Today." He listed the following traditional opposition forces to the government: the Socialist Party, the Communist Party, the Workers Committees, the Liberal Christian Democrats, and the Liberal Monarchists. He concluded his speech by indicating that Spain's problem was not the succession of Franco, but the distribution of power among the various forces representing the public.[25] The problem is thus a topic for public discussion and is printed in the daily press.

It is unlikely that General Franco will retain his control over the country very much longer. The concern is what will happen when he dies or is no longer able to govern the country. Many knowledgeable persons from the political left to the political right seem to feel that a peaceful transition will take place with only slight changes in basic existing policies. Along with the efficient police forces under military control, the army retains the ultimate power of Franco's regime and its loyalty to him is absolute.[26] If the political transition does take place without drastic policy changes, the army is likely to remain neutral. A coalition of a number of parties will rule, but with considerable political instability. In view of the uncertainties of the future, it is understandable why each of existing political organizations is attempting to build its strength now. The stronger an organization is at the time when Franco withdraws, the more power it will have to take over the government, by itself or in a coalition with others. The current political picture is one of instability and constant jockeying for power.

The Beginnings of Economic Planning

That the Spanish economy had made only little economic progress in the immediate postwar years was probably to be expected. According to one source,[27] the syndicalist framework of Franco Spain was inimical to rapid economic growth. The system favored and sheltered the least efficient enterprises and workers: external competition was limited by high tariffs and quotas, there was little pressure on workers to develop industrial discipline or to become geographically mobile, and foreign firms were deterred from investing.

By the end of 1958 Spain's economic situation was precarious, especially in reference to its foreign exchange reserves. It was evident to the new government that drastic measures were required, and in July 1959 the government drew up a stabilization program in cooperation with OEEC and the International Monetary Fund. The purpose of the 1959 Stabilization Plan was to lay the foundations of a balanced development as well as take the first steps toward integration in the European economy.[28] The Plan provided for a reduction in public expenditures and increases in certain taxes and in prices of state monopoly products. In the commercial field Spain undertook to liberalize trade. It fixed the rate of exchange with the dollar at sixty pesetas, adopted more liberal regulations regarding foreign investment, and introduced a new customs tariff. It also made efforts to promote free competition at home.[29] These decisions marked an end of economic isolation and cleared the way for a freer economy, based on international trade and economic cooperation with other countries.[30]

The immediate impact of the stabilization program was a slow-down of the economy. But the down-turn was temporary as readjustments took place. Starting in 1961 the stabilization program began showing success, to some degree because of the favorable influence of exceptional harvests in 1959 and the spectacular expansion of exports.[31] In addition the private sector was apparently convinced that the government plan did mean less regulation of, and less intervention in, the functioning of the private market.[32] Trade was progressively liberalized, some price controls removed, and a greater freedom given to both domestic and foreign investment. Forces of competition emerged again, and after a long interval manufacturers were concerned as much with markets as with production.[33]

Success of the stabilization program depended to some extent upon the acceptance by labor of a wage stabilization policy. Continued rapid inflation could undermine the total program. Largely through the sindicatos Spain integrated labor into the economic policy-making processes, and in general the formal labor leadership was willing to accept the set of rules, including the important premise that inflationary wage pressures were in no one's best interest. However, Spain did maintain in reserve its process of suppression of dissenting labor leaders. It is possible that the outlet of emigration saved Spain from more volatile and unexpected effects of stabilization. The effect of emigration was something of a surprise, particularly in its magnitude, and it was officially encouraged.[34]

The apparent success of the stabilization policies gave the government encouragement for further planning. Real national income per capita had increased by 9.7 percent in 1962, 12.4 percent in 1963, and 7.7 percent in 1964.[35] Through the efforts of various Ministries and special ad hoc committees, a Commission for Economic and Social Development Planning presented to the government a development plan for 1964-1967, which was approved on December 28, 1963.[36] In general the Plan was mandatory for the public sector but was intended only as a guide for the private sector, which was still operating principally under a price system. It followed the overall form of French planning which was basically indicative in nature. The Spanish Plan covered four years and set as a fundamental goal a 6 percent annual growth rate, or approximately 5 percent per capita, and annual productivity increases of about 5 percent. Consumption was to increase by 5.5 percent per year in the private sector and by 5 percent in the public sector. Imports were to increase by 9 percent, exports by 10 percent, and tourism by 11 percent per year. In the social field the Plan provided for the creation of 970,000 new jobs in industry and services, representing an increase of about 15 percent of the labor force.[37] Most of these projections were targets based upon "extrapolation from trends in the 1954-62 period, checked against European experience and against such target criteria as balance-of-payments equilibrium, economic stability, and full employment."[39]

During the first three years of the four-year Plan, the Spanish economy showed a strong and steady expansion. The annual rate of increase of real GNP exceeded the 6 percent rate forecast in the 1964-67 Plan, and other economic measures also showed significant gains. (See table 1 for various growth measures.) The expansion began slowing down in the latter part of 1966, and by the end of 1967 economic activity had probably fallen below the level of the year earlier. Unemployment had risen, while prices continued to rise because of substantial increases in labor costs.

The second economic plan was scheduled to go into effect in January, 1968, but because of the economic downturn in 1967 the start of the plan was delayed. There was concern about its acceptability by the public. The economy was relatively stagnant during much of 1968, but it showed a recovery in the fall, when minimum wage rates were increased and the wage freeze abolished. The upturn in economic activity that began in the second half of 1968 continued at a high rate in 1969, pointing to a rise in real GNP of about 8 percent from 1968 to 1969.[39]

The second development plan did not come into force until February 12, 1969, and its targets were lower than those of the first plan. In order to avoid inflation the annual growth rate of GNP was limited to 5.5 percent (3 percent for agriculture, 6.7 percent for industry, and 5 percent for the services sector). The plan retained its indicative character as regards the private sector, and concentrated on a careful investment policy rather than on increasing production.

TABLE 1

ANNUAL RATES OF GROWTH IN THE INDUSTRIAL SECTOR, 1964-1968

	Percentage of Growth over Preceding Year					Total Cumulated Growth	Average Annual Rate
	1964	1965	1966	1967	1968		
Physical Production	13.0	9.9	10.7	5.6	4.5	51.7	8.7
GNP at constant prices	13.4	9.4	9.3	4.5	4.5	48.1	8.2
GNP at current prices	18.0	14.1	12.6	7.3	5.6	71.8	11.4
Prices of industrial products	4.1	4.3	3.0	2.7	1.1	16.0	3.0
Total employment	4.7	4.1	4.0	1.6	0.7	16.0	3.0
Man-hours worked	4.6	4.1	4.0	0.9	0.0	14.4	2.7
Productivity per employee	8.3	5.1	5.1	2.8	3.8	27.7	5.0
Productivity per hour of work	8.4	5.1	5.1	3.6	4.5	29.5	5.3
Total Cost of personnel	18.2	19.7	19.4	16.7	9.5	115.9	16.6
Cost per hour of work	12.9	14.9	14.9	15.7	9.5	88.7	13.5

Source: Ministry of Industry, *Report on Industry in 1967 and 1968*, as quoted in Banco de Bilbao, *Informe económica*, 1968, p. 117.

To a large degree, especially in the private sector, the economic plans of Spain gave the principal responsibility for regulating growth to the market. While government action was indicated in the Plans, such action was to be used as a guide, or as a corrective factor, for the free market. The market mechanism in Spain, however, has not functioned freely, nor as an efficient allocator of resources and income. In an oblique comment, an official report of the sindicatos criticized the role given to the market by the economic plans, and noted that a high degree of monopoly in many sectors made the role of the market even less efficient as a coordinator of growth.[40]

The period from 1959 through 1969 brought many significant changes to Spain, and the improvement in the per capita income was marked. Spain was succeeding in its efforts to draw closer to the standards of living that were common to the other Western European nations. The planning during this period did open to debate the question of the nation's priority: economic planning for greater levels of production or social planning for greater equality and social justice. The government was in the hands of those who gave top priority to economic growth and development.

The First and Second Economic Plans

The basic overall planning in Spain is done by the Commission of Planning for Economic and Social Development, located in the Office of the Presidency. A single Commissioner, with Minister status, directs the staff and develops the overall philosophy and policies of the planning organization. To put together a specific plan a series of boards and committees are established, with representatives from government

agencies, business organizations and the academic. The planning commission's staff economicsts are assigned to each board and committee
as secretaries, and they do most of the technical work that is needed. In
general, these economists set the scope and the targets for the boards
and committees.

The scope of the first economic plan was comprehensive, and aimed
primarily at the basic issues of productivity generation. The emphasis
was on sheer economic growth. As stated in Article 1 of the Decree
which approved the Plan and its scope:[41]

> The purpose of the Plan is to raise the standard of all Spaniards,
> in conformity with the demands of social justice, and to ensure
> the growth of freedom and the dignity of the individual.

In spelling out its specific objectives, the Plan states that the primary
objective is to produce the largest possible volume of goods and services required in a competitive market while maintaining quality and
equitable pricing. Listed under this price objective are the following
elements.[42]

1. Maximum growth of GNP: attainment of the highest possible
level of goods and services
2. Equitable distribution of income: distribution of goods and services in an increasingly more equitable manner
3. Flexibility of the economic system: guarantee of freedom of choice
to consumers, workers and businessmen
4. Economic equilibrium: avoidance of excess production that
would result in price rises or a negative effect on the balance of payments
5. Full employment: complete and effective utilization of labor,
with adequate vocational training
6. Progressive integration into the world economy.

The plan and its provisions were made binding on the public sector, but
not on the private sector for which the plan was indicative. Of the total
economic activity in manufacturing, commerce and agriculture, it is
estimated that only about 10 percent is in the hands of the government,
and thus relatively little was covered by mandatory planning. In the
public sector, involving general public administration and public
services (i.e., schools, both building and teaching, road building,
police, etc.) planning did have an impact because it was mandatory and
specific.

Based upon overall data for the economy, the first plan looks successful. According to Planning Minister Laureano López Rodó, the targets
set by the first plan (in real terms) were readily met:[43]

PERCENT OF ANNUAL INCREASE

	Forecast	Realized
GNP	6.0	6.3
Imports	9.0	12.1
Private Consumption	5.5	6.0
Public Consumption	5.0	5.3
Gross Fixed Capital Formation	9.0	10.2
Exports	10.5	11.2

Although there is no basis on which to question the accuracy of the statistics, many persons in and out of the government feel that the Spanish economy grew during the mid-1960s despite the plan. One critic notes that the rate of growth in 1964, the first year of the plan, was slower than in previous years, and he points out that the target of an annual growth rate of 6 percent is not significant, since the Spanish economy had developed at a much higher rate in 1962 and 1963 without indicative planning.[44] In the same vein, the plan was criticized for not being sufficiently indicative for the private sector, since the economic activity in a large number of subsectors departed widely from the forecasts; and precisely in the two sectors which gave the greatest impulse to the Spanish economy in 1964—tourism and construction—is where the difference between reality and forecast has been large.[45]

Other comments critical of the plan's results were also made. In analyzing the accomplishments of the plan, the Organizacion Sindical listed the following comments:

1. While the GNP grew in the period of planning at an annual cumulative rate of 6.3 percent, which exceeded slightly the plan's projection, the "success" is an arithmetic coincidence; in 1965 the increase was 7.6 percent, in 1966 it was 7.4 percent and in 1967 it did not reach 4 percent.
2. The plan foresaw an annual increase of gross fixed capital of 9 percent in real terms; but it was 21.4 percent in 1965; 12.6 percent in 1966; and -4.4 percent in 1967.
3. The intersectoral population movement was much more intense than forecast; while agriculture lost some 450,000 active individuals in the period, the forecast was 340,000.[46]

Spain's economy did make significant advances on many fronts during the four-year period of the first plan. To what degree these gains were the result of economic planning is a moot point. According to Minister of Planning López Rodó, the basic achievement of the first plan was "the creation in Spain of a 'development' state of mind. Today this mental attitude is well entrenched, not only in cities and industrial centers, but also in the country. A desire has arisen to improve one's own living conditions and to cooperate in the general expansion of the economy."[47] There is little doubt that such a psychological factor may be important to the long-run possibilities of rapid development.

Plan II, scheduled to cover the years 1968-71 inclusive, was put into effect a year late because of the marked decline in economic activity in 1967 and 1968. While the first plan was comprehensive in scope and emphasized sheer economic growth, the second plan was selective and showed some concern about the economic allocation of resources and the need to increase the competitiveness of the economy. The strategy was to eliminate the obstacles to growth in the Spanish economy, while giving high priorities to agriculture and education, with more limited emphasis on public housing, urban planning, and revision in the social security system. The plan also specified six economic indicators as "alert signals," which were designed to indicate the permissable deviations from the specific objectives of the Plan. As shown on table 2, the growth targets are substantial, but not as great as in the first plan.

TABLE 2

Economic Plan for 1968-1971
(in thousands of millions of Ptas)

| | 1967 | Percent Growth-Annual Cumulative Average | | 1971 | |
		Real Terms	Money Terms	Ptas of 1967	Ptas of 1971
GNP	1,616.5	5.5	8.3	2,002.6	2,223.8
Imports	237.2	6.6	11.7	308.6	363.9
Available Resources	1,853.7			2,311.2	2,587.7
Private Consumption	1,142.2	4.5	7.5	1,362.0	1,528.7
Public Consumption	160.4	3.4	9.1	185.2	227.8
Capital Formation	369.8	6.9	9.0	482.9	523.1
Exportation	181.3	11.8	14.1	283.1	283.1
Utilization of Resources	1,853.7			2,311.2	2,587.7

Source: Plan II, p. 100.

References to manpower were made in the second Plan as it discussed the issues of productivity and employment. The Plan assumed that production would grow at the rate of 3.9 percent for the whole economy. This implies the creation of a million new jobs in the industrial and service sectors, while some 420,000 persons will have to abandon the agricultural sector. A basic assumption was that the unemployment rate of 2 percent would remain unchanged, and that total employment, therefore, would rise by 1.25 percent per year, which is the growth rate of the labor force.

Among the many boards and committees which issued reports to the Planning Commission, the Board on Labor did little on manpower planning.[48] The report of this committee did recognize the importance of the goal of equilibrium between manpower resources and the demand for manpower. However, little was proposed on how to attain this goal. In general, the attitude seems to have been that in early stages of planning (both Plans I and II) there is little need for detail, and that manpower planning involves details that were unnecessary for Spain at that stage of her economic development.[49]

III

The Labor Market Scene
Demand for Labor

The functioning of labor markets in a nation may vary according to geography, industry, or occupation. When comparing countries, however, the factors that differentiate labor markets are customs and institutions. And here, Spain's history and its more recent experience at isolation and autarky have had their impact on the labor markets of the country. One example may indicate the effects of tradition and institutions.

Until about 1950 to 1955 there were relatively few jobs open in the private sector of Spain for university graduates, and those that were open went to relatives of bureaucrats and to those with connections. It has been estimated that about 90 percent of university graduates were interested in and went into some type of government job, a figure that may currently be down to 80 or 85 percent. Government employment gave job security, and security was and perhaps still is very important in terms of social patterns. While social customs are undoubtedly going through a change at present, until recently marriage was possible only if one had a secure job. The most secure jobs were available in the public sector, and it was not too uncommon for university graduates to spend from three to seven years studying for specific civil service exams.

The attitude toward unemployment is another indicator of the functioning of labor markets. According to one study[1] where industrial workers were asked about the possibility of finding work in the event of unemployment, 26 percent indicated they would have average difficulty, 33 percent said it would be easy, and 38 percent said difficult. The response by agriculture workers was not markedly different. Twenty-five percent indicated average difficulty; 37 percent said easy; and 35 percent said difficult. Of the industrial workers who did not think they would have a difficult time in finding employment, 37 percent indicated they would find a job in manufacturing, 35 percent in construction, and 9 percent in agriculture. Of the agricultural workers who did not think they would have a difficult time finding employment, 78 percent indicated they would find work in agriculture, 14 percent in construction, and 9 percent in manufacturing.

General Working Rules

The day-to-day operation of the labor markets in Spain is affected in numerous ways by the rules developed directly and indirectly by the Organizacion Sindical.[2] The Organizacion Sindical is composed of twenty-eight national sindicatos, each of which covers a certain branch of activity. Within these sindicatos, employers and workers are grouped in different sections, the employers' section known as the "economic" section, and the workers' section as the "social" section. The existence in each sindicato of these two sections raises the problem of possible interference by one section in the other's affairs, and the possible interference by the State in the affairs of either sector.[3] Membership is obligatory for all persons except government employees who receive a wage or salary.

Collective bargaining of a limited nature does take place, and the process does extend to the strike, which technically is not illegal when limited to economic issues. In the past few years the strike has been used more and more, as workers refuse to accept the terms offered at the bargaining table. At present collective agreements have become the basic instrument for determining conditions of work. It has been estimated that by the end of 1967 out of a total of about 6.7 million wage earners 73 percent were covered by collective agreements or binding regulations laid down by the authorities in the absence of agreement between the parties.[4]

Expenses in connection with occupational accidents and diseases are met entirely from employers' contributions. Social security, however, is financed by contributions from workers, employers, and the state. An employer contributes 42 percent and a worker 8 percent of what amounts to the legal minimum wage. Since the minimum wage is considerably less than actual earnings of the average worker, social security benefits are therefore relatively low. However, the relatively high costs of fringes to the employer undoubtedly have some effect on the demand for additional workers.

Spanish workers have a relatively high degree of security in their jobs, but under specified conditions employers may discharge an employee. A discharge is justified for repeated absenteeism or chronic lateness; refusal to abide by labor regulations; extreme disrespect toward the employer; worker's inability to do the job for which he was recruited; and frequent unwarranted fights with other workers. If a worker is dismissed for justifiable reason, he is not entitled to compensation or reinstatement on his job.

If an employer finds himself in financial difficulty, he must file with the Ministry of Labor for approval to discharge some or all of his employees. Depending upon the circumstances, the labor authorities may (1) turn down the employer's pleas to be allowed to shut down temporarily or permanently; (2) authorize dismissal or suspension of all or part of the work force; or (3) call for a reduction in wages, length of the workday, etc. If workers are dismissed, they may receive up to a year's wages, depending on length of service. Older workers may speed up their retirement age by five years.

The government has developed a program to foster the movement of workers to areas of labor shortages. If a person from an underdeveloped area of the country wants to move to another area where jobs are available, and if he has a contract for a job in the latter area, the government will pay the transportation for him and his family, and will also give him a small allowance to help him settle in the new area. If he locates the job through the employment service, the service arranges for his transportation and allowances. If he obtains the job on his own, he must file a request with the Ministry of Labor for the transportation and allowances. An administrative decision is made whether the move qualifies for government assistance.[5]

Minimum Wages and Wage Rates

In the past few years there has been increased pressure on wages, primarily as a result of the big harvest of 1968, the comparatively low level of unemployment (approximately 2 percent, according to official statistics), and the general rise in economic activity without the concomitant increase in the required industrial manpower. Since the pressure on the wages of skilled workers seems relatively greater, it would appear that the shortage of skilled workers is probably greater than that of other workers.[6]

The pressure on salaries has not been in existence for too many years. It was only in 1963 that a minimum wage was established for the first time. In that year the daily minimum wage was set at 60 pesetas,[7] and it has been estimated that about two million workers were affected by the establishment of that rate.[8] In October, 1966, the minimum was increased by 40 percent to 84 pesetas, whereas the cost of living had only increased by 35 percent. Despite this apparent gain, a survey on minimum daily budgets for October, 1966, indicated that a family of two adults and two children in Madrid needed a daily income of 211 pesetas to live.[9] In January, 1969, the daily minimum wage was increased to 102 pesetas, and then adjusted upward to 120 pesetas a day in March, 1970.[10] At about that time it was estimated that a family of four needed 305 pesetas a day in order to live.[11]

Early in 1970 average net earnings of industrial workers was approximately 250 pesetas a day. The blue-collar worker was paid by the day, but if he were a regular full-time employee he received pay for thirty days a month, thirteen months a year. The range in earnings among occupations and industries was wide. The mineworkers in northern Spain, for example, earned about 700 pesetas daily,[12] or the equivalent of 10 dollars a day.

As shown in table 3, there is not a single minimum wage, but a series of such wages, for different occupational groups. There is an interoccupational structure with fixed relationships, and these relationships are retained when the minimum wages are raised. The earnings of almost all workers other than unskilled are above the minimum for their classification. These minimum rates do have some significance since they are used as the base to compute social security deductions and sindicato levies.

The earnings of Spanish workers are normally composed of a basic wage plus various allowances, and in many cases the supplementary payments are almost as much as the basic salary. These supplementary allowances may include the following:[13]

1. Extraordinary payments, which generally have no direct relation to the work done. These would include extra payments at Christmas and on July 18, and increments paid as a result of seniority.
2. Productivity bonuses, including such bonuses for punctuality, for good behavior, etc.
3. Family allowances.
4. Miscellaneous allowances, including cost-of-living allowances and residential benefits.

During 1965, the second year of the first economic plan, both wholesale prices and the cost-of-living index rose sharply, at rates about three times those that occurred in 1964. The rise of 10 percent in wholesale prices and of 13 percent in the cost-of-living index was seen by the government as a threat to the success of the economic plan. In February 1966 a wage adjustment ceiling of 8 percent per year was imposed in an effort to dampen down the inflationary pressures. Because the wage ceiling was applicable only to the basic wage and not to the wage allowances, the effort to constrain wages, and also prices, could only be partially successful. Many collective agreements exceeded the 8 percent, and the government authorities called upon the bargaining committees to reconsider the agreements in order to ensure that there were no adverse impacts on prices. Practically all were approved, after a certain delay, once the authorities were assured that a price increase would not be made.[14] As shown in table 4, wage increases far exceeded the movement of wholesale prices and of the cost of living index.

The Spanish economy slowed down markedly in 1967, as its balance of payments worsened. When Britain devalued the pound in November, 1967, Spain devalued the peseta by the equivalent percentage, from 60 to 70 pesetas per dollar. And in order to dampen the wage and price situation, Spain froze wages, suspended collective bargaining, and imposed limited price controls. Despite the freeze earnings of workers continued to rise in 1968, principally from adjustments in fringe benefits and family allowances, but at a much slower rate than in the previous two years. The rise in the cost of living also slowed down markedly.

TABLE 3

SPANISH MINIMUM WAGE SCALES, 1967

Occupational Group	Grade Level	Minimum Wage			
		Monthly Rate		Daily Rate	
		Pesetas	Dollars[2]	Pesetas	Dollars[2]
Professionals (Titulados)	grade 1	5,670	81.00	189	2.70
	grade 2	4,770	68.00	159	2.27
Managers (Jefes)	grade 3	3,960	57.00	132	1.88
Foremen (Administrativos y capataces)	grade 4	3,420	49.00	114	1.63
	grade 5	3,150	45.00	105	1.50
Assistant Foremen (Subalternos y auxiliares)	grade 6	2,610	37.00	87	1.24
	grade 7	2,520	36.00	84	1.20
Skilled (Oficiales)	grade 8	—	—	96	1.37
Semi-Skilled (Especialistas)	grade 9	—	—	90	1.28
Unskilled[1] (Peones)	grade 10	—	—	84	1.20
Apprentices, 3rd & 4th year (Aprendizes)	grade 11	—	—	56	0.80
Apprentices, 1st & 2nd year (Aprendizes)	grade 12	—	—	35	0.50

1. The minimum wage for the unskilled worker is the one normally quoted as *the* minimum wage.
2. Dollar figures were calculated by converting the pesetas at the official exchange rate of 70 pesetas to the dollar. Source: Sociedad de Investigaciones Económicas, *Modelo econométrico de política laboral (1954-1971)*, Tomo 1, 1967, p. 195.

The effects of the recovery on employment and unemployment began to be felt in the spring of 1968. Pressures began building up in the labor market, and when the wage freeze came to an end in October, 1968, new guidelines were established, permitting basic wage rates to increase by 5.9 percent in collective wage agreements concluded in 1969. Again, hourly earnings continued to rise much faster than this, due at least in part that increases from better fringe benefits, seniority, or productivity improvements were not covered by the guidelines.[15]

On January 1, 1970, the 5.9 percent wage guidelines were superseded by the following rules: wage settlements should take into account, as the main criteria, the productivity increase, the general economic situation, and the time period covered by the agreement; (b) collective agreements would require governmental approval whenever "the real economic repercussions resulting from the wage increases or from other stipulated conditions would be above 8 percent in agreements covering two or more years." It was further established that for those agreements covering two or more years a sliding scale adjustment could be applied. Concerning prices, the controls established in November, 1967, were maintained, and essential food imports continued to be subsidized.[16]

TABLE 4

PERCENTAGE CHANGES IN PRICES
AND WAGES, 1960-1968

Price and Wage Indices	Weights	Annual Increases				December to October	
		Average 1960 to 1967	1966	1967	1968	1968	1969
A WHOLESALE PRICES:							
1 General index	100	4.0	2.6	0.5	2.3	0.0	1.6
of which:							
2 Food, drink and tobacco Special Groups	52	5.5	3.1	0.3	3.1	-0.1	0.8
3 Agricultural product	34	5.4	4.4	-0.9	3.2	-0.7	1.9
4 Processed agricultural products	12	4.4	0.4	4.6	2.6	0.6	-0.7
5 Industrial products	30	1.9	1.3	1.2	0.1	2.4	
B COST-OF-LIVING:							
1 General index	100	6.8	6.2	6.4	4.9	1.5	1.4
2 Food	49	6.7	4.5	3.8	4.5	2.0	1.1
3 Clothing and footwear	14	8.9	9.7	11.5	4.1	0.0	2.4
4 Rent	8	6.0	7.9	8.8	6.8	1.3	1.1
5 Household expenses	10	4.9	4.1	4.4	3.3	0.6	0.2
6 Other goods and services	19	6.6	9.7	10.5	7.0	1.6	2.5
C WAGES:							
1 Hourly labour costs in manufacturing:							
(a) Inst. of Stat. (Sindicatos)		15.0	17.6	15.3	8.7	9.9[2]	11.4[2]
(b) Ministry of Industry		15.2[1]	15.9	14.5	10.1	—	—
2 Hourly labour costs in construction		14.4[1]	12.1	14.0	8.1	—	—
3 Agricultural wages			14.7	11.0	7.9	9.9[3]	8.8[3]

1. Average 1961 to 1967.
2. Last November to September.
3. November to November.
Source: National Institute of Statistics, Ministry of Industry and of Agriculture, as
    quoted in OECD, *Economic Surveys: Spain*, January 1970, p. 17.

Changes in Earnings

Since the adoption of policies to foster rapid economic growth, Spain's government has been concerned about inflation, labor productivity, and wage-price relationships. The second economic plan did establish the principle that salary adjustments ought not to exceed the productivity increases, and that the minimum salary would be revised annually as a function of the rise in the cost of living.[17] Real hourly earnings of workers have risen significantly, although not uniformly, among the different economic sectors. As shown on table 5, in 1963 only one industry, banking and insurance, had more than 50 percent of its employees earning over 60,000 pesetas annually. In 1968 there were three economic sectors with more than half their employees earning in excess of 60,000 pesetas, and over the five-year period most sectors nearly doubled the percent of workers earning at that level. For all industries the increase was from 17.2 percent in 1963 to 31.2 percent in 1968 for workers earning more than 60,000 pesetas; and for those earning less than 24,000 pesetas, the decline was from 21.2 percent in 1963 to 11.0 percent in 1968.

Average hourly earning in selected industries have shown wide ranges of increases during the past few years. In the first quarter of 1967 average hourly earnings ranged from a low of 18.05 pesetas for shoes, clothing, and leather to a high of 46.28 pesetas for banking. Surprising is the low earnings in construction. (See appendix table III-I.) For most industries increases in 1968 exceeded 10 percent, with banking showing the largest. Increases in 1969 were less uniform, with a few industries showing increases of less than 10 percent. The differentials between the unskilled and the skilled varied significantly among the industries, ranging from a high of 82 percent in printing and publishing, to a low of 38 percent in commerce.

TABLE 5

DISTRIBUTION OF WAGE AND SALARY INCOME, IN
CONSTANT PESETAS OF 1963, BY ECONOMIC SECTOR
(Percentage of total wage and salary employees)

Economic Sector	Annual Income of More Than 60,000 Pesetas ($1,000)		Annual Income of 24,000 to 60,000 Pesetas ($400 to $1,000)		Annual Income of less than 24,000 Pesetas ($400)	
	1963	1968	1963	1968	1963	1968
Banking and Insurance	64.2	69.6	27.3	24.8	8.5	5.6
Electricity and gas	37.0	63.1	57.5	34.5	5.5	2.4
Mining	28.9	52.9	62.6	43.4	8.5	3.7
Durable Goods Industries	23.0	39.8	61.7	52.1	15.3	8.1
Consumer Goods Industries	10.6	20.6	64.1	63.9	25.3	15.5
Commerce	12.8	22.9	54.2	59.8	33.0	17.3
Construction	5.8	17.9	65.4	70.4	28.8	11.7
Total	17.2	31.2	61.6	57.8	21.2	11.0

Sources: Instituto Nacional de Estadística, *Informe sobre la distribución de las rentas, Año 1968* (Madrid, 1969), p. 64.
Note: In 1963 the official exchange rate was 60 pesetas to the dollar.

Examining the income changes of all nonagricultural workers, by occupational category, shows marked gains in real terms for each group over the five-year period 1963-1968. (See table 6.) While more than three-quarters of the semiskilled and unskilled workers earned less than 15 pesetas per hour in 1963, the percentage dropped to under 50 in 1968, in real terms. At the higher income, of more than 40 pesetas per hour, the engineers and other professionals were represented by 70 percent in

TABLE 6

PERCENTAGE OF WORKERS RECEIVING DESIGNATED HOURLY EARNINGS
(excluding Family Allowances, 1963-1968)

Occupational Category[3]	Under 15 Pesetas ($0.25)[1]			From 15 to 40 Pesetas			More than 40 Pesetas ($0.67)[1]		
	1963	1968 in current Pesetas	1968 in constant 1963 Pesetas[2]	1963	1968 in current Pesetas	1968 in constant 1963 Pesetas[2]	1963	1968 in current Pesetas	1968 in constant 1963 Pesetas[2]
I. Engineers and other Professionals	—			30.4	0.1	16.4	69.6	99.9	83.6
II. Technicians	—			83.8	5.6	53.5	16.2	94.4	46.5
III. Foremen and other administrators	19.5	0.1	5.0	73.8	53.6	75.4	6.7	46.3	19.6
IV. Skilled Workers	31.6	0.6	7.0	68.4	85.2	91.0	—	14.2	2.0
V. Semiskilled, Unskilled and apprentices	77.6	13.7	44.8	22.4	80.4	54.9	—	5.9	0.3
Total	49.7	5.8	21.2	47.3	73.6	71.4	3.0	20.6	7.4

1. Converted at 1963 official rate of 60 pesetas to the dollar.
2. Corrected by the cost of living index.
3. Occupational titles frequently lose meaning in translation, because of the specialized meanings in a foreign country. The following are the five groups, as listed in Spanish:
    I. Técnicos titulados: Ingenieros y licenciados; peritos y ayudantes.
    II. Técnicos sin titular: Técnicos de oficina, laboratorio y taller.
    III. Administrativos: Jefes, oficiales, auxiliaries, aspirentes y subalternos.
    IV. Obreros cualificados: Jefes de equipo y oficiales.
    V. Peones y aprendices: Peones (especializados y ordinarios) y aprendices.

Source: Instituto Nacional de Estadística, Informe sobre la distribución de las rentas, Año 1968, (Madrid, 1969), pp. 66-67.

1963 and 84 percent in 1968 (in real terms). Substantial gains were made by the technicians (from 16 percent to 46 percent), and by the foremen and other administrators (from 7 percent to 20 percent). What appears to be of special interest are the substantial differences between the earnings of the blue-collar groups, and of the supervisory and while-collar groups. In 1968 about half the foremen and almost all of the technicians and professionals earned in excess of the 40 pesetas, but less than 15 percent of the skilled workers and about 6 percent of the other blue-collar workers earned that amount. While all groups of workers have improved their economic status over time, the lower salaried workers have not improved their position significantly in relation to the higher salaried workers.

The average hourly earnings of the various occupational groups of Spanish workers have increased regularly from year to year, but the levels are still relatively low. The average hourly earnings of all non-agricultural workers in 1963 was 16.81 pesetas, ranging from a low of 12.79 pesetas for the semiskilled and unskilled group to 54.90 pesetas for the engineers and other professionals; and the former group was 25 percent less than the average while the latter group was two and a fourth times larger than the average. By 1968 the hourly earnings of the average worker was 31.44 pesetas, almost double that of 1963. The earnings of the lowest paid group was 24.54 pesetas and of the highest, 81.52 pesetas; the former had made some relative advance and was only 22 percent less than the average while the latter group had sustained a relative loss and was only about one and a half times larger than the average.

The average annual change over the period 1963 to 1968 was relatively similar for each of the occupational categories, with three groups —the skilled, the foremen, and the technicians—at about a 12 percent annual increase. The semiskilled and unskilled group showed a slightly higher raise (13.9 percent), while the professional group showed the lowest with 8.2 percent. The pattern of changes by year showed much wider ranges. In the 1963-1964 period the semiskilled and unskilled group obtained a 15.9 percent increase, while the other increases were between 3 and 7 percent. The following year it was the skilled group that outdistanced the others, with a gain of 24.2 percent. And in 1966-1967 it was the technicians with a gain of 21 percent that showed the largest gains. Thus while the pattern seems erratic, the occupational groups did gain about the same relative amounts over the five-year period. In 1969 average hourly earnings for all workers 35.12 pesetas.[18] This gain of 11.7 percent was significantly higher than the increase during 1968, the year of the wage freeze, but substantially lower than in the three previous years.

In 1963 about one-fifth of the wage earners earned less than 24,000 pesetas annually, and they had 8.7 percent of all income; and at the other extreme of the scale, 1.6 percent of the workers earned more than

120,000 pesetas annually, and they had 6.1 percent of all income. By 1968 all incomes had risen substantially, but the distribution had not changed markedly. Because of the intervals of salary ranges it is not possible to obtain the identical percentage of workers for two separate years. In 1963 17.2 percent of the workers earned more than 60,000 pesetas annually, and they received 34.8 percent of all income; in 1968, 17.7 percent of the workers earned more than 108,000 pesetas annually, and they received 36.2 percent of all income. Relatively little redistribution of income among wage earners occurred over the five-year period.

Overall distribution of income has changed moderately, in favor of the wage and salary workers. In 1954 total wages and salaries represented 54.6 percent of Spain's national income; by 1959 the proportion rose to 57.2 percent. National income per capita was 51,679 pesetas (or 738 dollars) in 1969, a rise of 9 percent over the 47,378 pesetas (or 676 dollars) in 1968.[19] On January 22, 1971, the Spanish government announced that per capita national income in 1970 reached an estimated $818 and that its objective was to reach one thousand dollars by 1972, corresponding to an average rate of increase of 10.5 percent a year.[20]

General Employment Trends

The most direct measure of the demand side of the labor market is the total number of persons who are working, although job vacancies must be added to arrive at a more complete demand figure. However, as in most countries around the world, Spain has no statistics on job vacancies, and only partial and probably unreliable estimates of shortages of certain skills are available.

The concept of the labor force, i.e., población activa, is frequently used in Spain as though it were synonymous with employment, but technically the labor force includes both those who are working and those who are seeking work. Inasmuch as official unemployment rates are exceedingly low, i.e., about 2 percent or less,[21] the difference in the global figures for the labor force and for those employed is slight. Nevertheless, differences can be of some importance when dealing with specific segments of the labor force.

The first indication of the Franco government's concern with the overall operation of the labor market occurred in about 1964. Prior to that time scattered and not too efficient employment service offices existed, from which the official unemployment statistics were collected; and various vocational training programs were being offered, but they in no way reflected the needs of the market. Statistics such as wages, hours, and migration were collected by various organizations in and out of the government, but no effort was made to coordinate the activities and data, or to analyze what was happening.

While the first economic plan went into effect in 1964, various boards and committees were established by the Planning Commission in 1962 to study and report on specific industries and cross-industry problems. One such board was the Labor Board which did compile and study the relevant available statistics, and did present some forecasts on a global basis. The Plan, as finally adopted, did of course set full employment as a goal, with the employment in the agricultural sector scheduled to decline, and with employment in the secondary and tertiary sectors to increase. Forecasts were based upon assumed labor force participation rates for males and females, and while the statistical tables were labeled as labor force data, the discussion of the data assumed them to be employment statistics. In any event, it is clear that Plan I did not consider manpower planning as an item of importance.[22]

The focus on planning did arouse an interest in manpower in parts of the government outside the Planning Commission. In the Ministry of Labor an office concerned with employment, Dirección General de Empleo, began a study of the operation of Spanish labor markets and did develop what it called the dynamics of employment.[23] While the schema was a simple one, it did indicate an understanding of the relevant manpower factors:[24]

1. Total population—all Spaniards and foreign workers in Spain
2. Potential labor force—those who have the capacity to work (principally those over 13 years of age)
3. Labor force—those of the potential labor force who have the desire to work
4. Employed population—those of the labor force who have the opportunity to work in Spain
5. Unemployed population—those of the labor force who reside in Spain and do not have the opportunity to work
6. Emigrants—those of the labor force who do not reside in Spain.

The analyses of the two years for which such studies were done did take into account year-to-year changes in statistics for economic sectors, industries, geographic areas, and occupational levels. In 1966, however, a reorganization in the Ministry of Labor eliminated the program.

At about the same time that the Ministry of Labor began its studies of manpower, the central statistical agency of the government, Instituto Nacional de Estadística (hereafter referred to as INE) began plans for a quarterly sample survey of the labor force. The first such report[25] was for 1964, and INE has continued to publish such reports annually. The 1964 report included data for the second, third, and fourth quarters of the year. The 1965 report covered all quarters as well as the annual average. By 1967, however, the surveys were cut back to two per year, in the second and fourth quarters, and the data published from then on were for these two quarters as well as the annual average. The data are not published quarterly, when the statistics are collected, but released in annual reports, published considerably later than period covered.

For example, both the 1967 and 1968 reports were released at the same time, sometime at the end of 1969.

These INE reports contain detailed information on the Spanish labor force cross-classified by most factors relevant to the operation of the labor market, although information on job vacancies, which has to be collected from firms, is not available. The sample survey does not include (1) the cities of Ceuta and Melilla,[26] (2) persons in the military service, and (3) persons in collective homes, and therefore the various cross-classified statistics do not contain persons in these three groups. However, in the introduction of each of the yearly reports INE presents longitudinal statistics on what it refers to as the "total" labor force, i.e., including estimates of persons in the three groups omitted from the sample survey. While the differences are not large (about 2 to 3 percent), other sources, both government and nongovernment, quote INE reports without indicating which labor force statistics are being used. It may be noted that the labor force statistics of the *Dinámica del empleo en 1965* differed from either of the two INE estimates, and other sources have also quoted slightly different figures.

In an analysis of demand for labor in Spain, employment data by economic activity are available[27] as shown on table 7. Total employment (including self-employed as well as wage and salaried workers) rose from 11.6 million in 1960 to 12.3 million in 1968, an increase of 5.5 percent over the eight-year period. (Over the same period total employment in the United States rose by almost 16 percent.) This rise averaged out declines of 20 percent in agriculture and fishing, and 35 percent in mining, along with increases in excess of 30 percent for commerce and 30 percent for other services. Despite the decline in agriculture it still represents a significant proportion of total employment, i.e., 41 percent in 1960 and 31 percent in 1968. Next to agriculture, manufacturing was the largest industry group, and it showed an increase of 20 percent in employment over the eight-year period.

If we calculate the gross number of new jobs created over the eight-year period, by excluding the employment declines in agriculture and in mining, and by counting only the employment gains of all other industry groups, we arrive at a figure of 1,700,000 new jobs. This would represent about 15 percent of total 1960 employment and 26 percent of total employment minus agriculture and mining employment.

Wage and salary workers represent about three out of five persons employed, and the increase from 1960 to 1968 was slight. In agriculture wage and salary workers represented about 40 percent in 1960 and only 28 percent in 1968, and the numbers declined by over two-fifths. The number of self-employed in agriculture dropped only by about 5 percent. The major increase in wage and salary workers occurred in the manufacturing industries.

From another source, a forecast of employment in 1971 over 1966 shows a rise of 6.2 percent. During the five-year period agricultural

TABLE 7
TOTAL EMPLOYMENT AND NUMBER OF WAGE AND SALARY WORKERS, BY ECONOMIC ACTIVITY 1960 AND 1968
(in thousands)

Economic Activities	1960 Total Employed	1960 Wage and Salary Workers No.	1960 Percent of total employed	1968 Total Employed	1968 Wage and Salary Workers No.	1968 Percent of total employed	Change 1960 to 1968 Total Employed No.	Change Total Employed %	Change Wage and Salary Workers No.	Change Wage and Salary Workers %
Agriculture & fishing	4,855.8	1,946.9	40.09	3,849.9	1,091.2	28.34	-1005.9	-20.72	-855.7	-43.95
Mining	190.9	183.8	96.28	124.1	117.9	95.00	- 66.8	-34.99	- 65.9	-35.85
Manufacturing	2,606.7	2,009.0	77.07	3,172.7	2,636.6	83.10	566.0	21.71	627.6	31.24
Food	387.2	267.1	68.98	450.8	334.9	74.29	63.6	16.43	67.8	25.38
Textiles	585.6	352.0	60.10	657.8	455.5	69.24	72.2	12.33	103.5	29.40
Paper	109.8	99.8	90.89	141.3	131.5	93.06	31.5	28.69	31.7	31.76
Chemicals	170.8	158.4	92.74	217.8	207.2	95.13	47.0	27.52	48.8	30.61
Glass & Ceramics	149.5	131.9	88.22	186.0	168.5	90.59	36.5	24.41	36.6	27.75
Metal (excl. machinery)	413.9	349.8	94.51	514.3	456.8	88.81	100.4	24.26	107.0	30.59
Transport equipment	215.1	191.3	88.93	325.2	296.9	91.29	110.1	51.19	105.6	55.20
All other	391.3	292.9	74.85	421.9	345.0	81.77	30.6	7.82	52.1	17.79
Construction	797.0	704.1	88.34	1,016.9	906.7	89.16	209.9	27.59	202.6	28.77
Electricity, Water, Gas	76.8	75.0	97.65	88.2	85.9	97.39	11.4	14.84	10.9	14.53
Commerce	958.9	499.0	52.03	1,279.5	657.2	51.36	320.6	33.43	158.2	31.70
Transport & communication	542.4	435.7	80.32	624.3	491.4	78.71	81.9	15.10	55.7	12.78
Other services	1,612.4	1,316.4	81.64	2,124.4	1,746.3	82.20	512.0	31.75	429.9	32.66
TOTAL	11,640.9	7,169.9	61.59	12,280.0	7,733.2	62.97	639.1	5.49	563.3	7.86

Source: Instituto Nacional de Estadística, *Población activa en 1968*, (Madrid 1969), p. XIV.

employment was expected to decline by 14 percent, and would represent only 23 percent of total employment by 1971. In addition to agriculture, declines were expected in mining and in the manufacture of shoes and clothing. Largest increases were expected in food manufacturing, construction, and commerce.(See appendix table III-2.)

In most other aspects of labor demand, labor force rather than employment statistics are used. It is not possible to extract employment statistics from the labor force figures where the latter are classified by occupational groups, socioeconomic groups, professional status, hours of work, age, or secondary jobs. There is no alternative but to use labor force data as a proxy for the demand for labor.

While the growth of the total labor force has been steady, it has not been equal throughout Spain. In the majority of regions o the country, from 1962 to 1967, the labor force has been stable, and in some regions it has actually declined. In only the industrial regions of Barcelona, Madrid, and the Basque area has there been a growth in the labor force of 15 percent or more.[28]

The Demand for Labor

The demand for labor by an individual firm is normally in terms of persons with specific skills who can perform certain functions which the firm needs done in order to produce the goods or services it sells. Markets are so organized that a worker is labeled with an occupational title in order to have him easily identified by firms or industries competing for his services. Table 8 presents a distribution of the labor force by occupational groups[29] for 1964 and 1968. The two largest occupational groups are the farmers, fishermen and related workers, and the artisans and various production workers. The former represented 34 percent of the labor force in 1964 and 31.6 percent in 1968; the latter represented 28.7 percent in 1964 and 30.6 percent in 1968. Other large groups were salesmen (about 10 percent), and service, sports, and entertainment workers (about 8 percent). Significant declines over the four-year period occurred in the miners group (44 percent), and the unskilled workers group (10 percent). Large gains were made in the office employees' group and the professional group, indicating a significant growth in the demand for white collar workers with high and medium levels of education. In the blue-collar groups the expansion was in skilled and semiskilled workers categories, indicating a growing need for specialized vocational training.

Another classification of the labor force is by socioeconomic group. Of the non-farm groups, the largest declines from 1964 to 1968 were among the professions (generally self-employed) and company managers. Largest increases occurred among high and medium level employees (white-collar) and among skilled workers. This helps confirm the growing need for an expansion in higher education and in vocaional training. (See appendix table III-3.)

TABLE 8

LABOR FORCE BY OCCUPATIONAL GROUPS, 1964 AND 1968
(in thousands)

Occupational Groups	1964 Number	1964 Percent	1968 Number	1968 Percent	Change 1964-1968 Absolute	Change 1964-1968 Percent
TOTAL	11,707.6	100.0	12,277.3	100.0	569.7	4.87
Professional, technical and related workers	360.2	3.0	417.3	3.3	57.1	15.85
Administrators, & managers	110.0	1.0	109.3	0.8	- 0.7	-0.64
Office employees	697.1	6.0	838.5	6.8	141.4	20.28
Salesmen	1,100.4	9.4	1,268.2	10.3	167.8	15.25
Farmers, fishermen & related workers	4,028.5	34.4	3,884.3	31.6	-144.2	-3.58
Miners, quarrymen & others	191.7	1.6	107.0	0.8	- 84.7	-44.18
Transport & communications workers	461.7	4.0	540.7	4.4	79.0	17.11
Artisans & workers in various production processes	3,361.2	28.7	3,690.9	30.6	329.7	9.81
Excavation and dock workers	103.9	0.9	124.3	1.0	20.4	19.63
Unskilled workers, unclassified	172.3	1.5	155.3	1.3	- 17.0	-9.87
Service, sports & entertainment workers	947.2	8.1	1,006.8	8.2	59.6	6.29
Workers, NEC	74.5	0.6	38.8	0.3	- 35.7	-47.92
Armed forces	97.9	0.8	95.9	0.7	- 2.0	- 2.04

Source: Recalculated from data in Instituto Nacional de Estadística, *Población activa en 1964* (Madrid, 1965), pp. 182-133; and *Población activa en 1968* (Madrid, 1969), pp. 42-43.

The demand for labor is not constant over even a short period of time. Undoubtedly employment fluctuates from week to week and from month to month. Some firms and some industries may be expanding, while others are contracting. Such variations are generally ironed out over time, and year-to-year changes indicate the general trend of employment and of the demand for labor. That a shift in demand for labor has occurred is evident from the rather sharp decline in agricu' tural employment and the rise in industrial and service employment. Where in 1940 agriculture represented over 50 percent of the labor force, it dropped to about 25 percent in 1970 and is expected to decline to about 20 percent by 1975. By 1970 employment in both industry and services exceeded one-third of the labor force.

Because of the nature of various industries, many employ seasonal workers and also casual workers. Employment in such industries may fluctuate widely over short time periods, and the workers involved may work considerably less than full time. However, the overall amount of such work is relatively small. Employment in agriculture is more affected by seasonal employment than other industries, but only 2.7 percent of agricultural workers are affected. The percent of seasonal employment in commerce, manufacturing, and construction also is in excess of 1 percent but less than 2 percent. Casual work is greatest in the construction industry, but it affects about one-half of 1 percent of the workforce.

The largest proportion of the labor force is employees (over 60 percent), with the others distributed among entreprenuers, family help, and self-employed workers. From 1964 to 1968 there has been a 9 percent rise in persons working for others, while the number of self-employed workers declined by about 30 percent, a factor indicative of the increasing pace of the industrialization process. As one would expect, almost all of the teenage persons in the labor force are either employees or family help. However, over 50 percent of the entrepreneurs are in the 45- to 64-year old age group, while only about 30 percent of the employees are of that age. (See appendix table III-4.)

The most common scheduled workweek ranges from forty-five to forty-eight hours, but a significant percent of the labor force work forth-four or fewer hours (15 percent), while over one-third work in excess of forth-eight hours. Almost 15 percent of the total labor force work sixty or more hours a week, an indication of the rather strong demand for certain kinds of labor, while about 7 percent[30] work less than thirty hours, indicating a weak demand for other kinds of labor. (See appendix table III-5.)

According to another source there is a considerable amount of both overemployment and underemployment in Spain, as measured by average hours worked per week. The general standard is the eight-hour day and the forty-eight-hour week, and by these standards it would seem that overemployment is the more significant, as shown by the following statistics:[31]

	Percent of Workers			
Hours Worked per week	Blue-Collar Workers, Spain 1966	Blue-Collar Workers, Madrid 1967	Blue-Collar Workers, Madrid 1969	White-Collar Workers, Madrid 1969
under 40	7·	7	7	17
41-50	51	44	48	43
over 50	42	49	45	40

In view of the legal requirement to pay overtime hours at penalty rates, these figures tend to confirm the finding that there is a relatively strong demand for certain kinds or groups of labor.

While statistics are not available to specify the shortage occupations, there are indications[32] of a substantial shortage of teachers in secondary schools, principally in the science fields. All secondary school teachers must be university graduates, and in the state schools they must also pass stiff examinations equivalent to civil service exams. There probably also exist shortages of auto repair mechanics and other repairmen of various household equipment.

In some high-level professional occupations it has been common for years for persons to hold more than one job. In recent years, with the rather rapid expansion of economic activity and of industrialization, this practice has increased and has spread widely to various blue-collar skilled occupations. One study reports that in 1966 in all of Spain, about 19 percent of white-collar employees and 12 percent of blue-collar workers held more than one job; and in 1969 in Madrid the percentages were 25 percent and 17 percent.[33] The statistics for Madrid in 1969 show that the proportion of persons with more than one job rises with higher income level and with higher labor classification:[34]

Monthly Income (ptas)	Percent of Workers with more than one job
From 6,000 to 12,000	17
From 12,001 to 20,000	28
More than 20,000	25

Labor Category	Percent of Workers with more than one job
Blue-Collar Worker	17
Unskilled	15
Skilled	18
White-Collar Worker	25
Low-Level	21
High-Level	36

The opportunities for holding secondary jobs are greater for many groups of white-collar and professional workers than for blue-collar workers. Almost all government offices are only open until about 2:30 or 3:00 P.M. This gives the government employee the time to engage in various other economic activities, and many take advantage of this opportunity. Only where there is a conflict of interest is a government employee forbidden from accepting a second job. Banks, insurance companies, and other service companies also operate only in mornings, thereby giving their professional employees the time to hold second jobs. Many university faculty members engage in a whole range of consulting activities. Blue-collar workers have much less time for secondary employment, but many take on small private jobs such as painting, carpentry, plumbing, etc.

An indication of the amount of time spent on secondary employment is shown in table 9. Of the total who have more than one job, over 15 percent work 30 or more hours on their secondary job. Of the 31,800 who worked more than forty-eight hours on their primary job, about 13,000, or 40 percent worked 15 or more hours on other jobs. And 10 percent of those who worked sixty or more hours on their principal job worked thirty or more hours on secondary jobs. Again this seems to contribute to the evidence of a relatively heavy demand for certain skills and professions in the labor market.

TABLE 9

NUMBER OF PERSONS WITH A SECOND JOB, ACCORDING
TO WEEKLY HOURS WORKED IN EACH ACTIVITY, 1968
(in thousands)

Hours Worked in Principal Activity	Number of persons who, on secondary job, worked					
	Total	From 1 to 7 hours	From 8 to 14 hours	From 15 to 21 hours	From 22 to 29 hours	30 or more hours
TOTAL	232.9	21.5	66.6	70.1	37.5	37.2
From 0 to 14	13.5	1.5	1.8	0.6	1.7	7.9
From 15 to 29	24.5	1.8	4.1	6.8	6.6	5.2
From 30 to 39	46.6	2.4	9.7	12.8	11.8	9.9
From 40 to 44	32.9	2.7	8.5	13.1	4.4	4.2
From 45 to 48	83.6	7.1	29.6	28.7	10.7	7.5
From 49 to 54	18.2	3.1	7.3	5.2	1.1	1.5
From 55 to 59	2.8	0.5	1.1	1.2	—	—
60 or more	10.8	2.4	4.5	1.7	1.2	1.0

Source: Instituto Nacional de Estadística, Población activa en 1968, (Madrid, 1969), p. 59.

Another indication of the labor demand picture in Spain is the emigration situation. The migration of labor is clearly affected by the demand for labor (relative to the demand for similar types of labor in other countries), as well as the relative supply of labor. Because of the relatively heavy demand for labor in many western European countries during the 1950s and 1960s significant numbers of Spanish workers left for work abroad. Thus, according to the International Labor Office,[35] Spain's low unemployment figures are partly due to emigration to various countries in Western Europe, which helped stabilize the employment market. Net emigration to European countries, after deducting the number returning to Spain, reached a peak in 1961 with 108,000 persons, and then has declined constantly since. In 1969 it is estimated that the net emigration totaled about 25,000.[36] The cumulative total of emigration for the past ten years or so amounted to about 1,000,000 workers, or 8 percent of the labor force.

Data seem to indicate that a significant majority of emigrants to continental Europe had been engaged in agriculture and fishing while about 40 percent had been production workers and unskilled workers in industry.[37] It would thus appear that while the demand in the Spanish labor markets for selected professionals and skilled occupations has not been satisfied, a substantial part of the surplus of agricultural and unskilled industrial labor emigrated to Western European countries where the demand for unskilled labor was high.

IV

Manpower Supply and Targets

In its broadest terms, the supply of manpower may be considered as a stock of individuals with specific skills, at specific points of time. On the market place these individuals must make decisions on the amount of labor (hours of work) they are prepared to give at the wage rates being offered by firms. And an analysis of supply involves not only the composition of the stock, but the flow of persons entering and of those leaving the stock.

A simplistic view of the stock of manpower is the labor force at a specific period of time, although it must be understood that labor force participation can readily expand or contract from an existing stock of the population. Thus, in 1968 the labor force participation rate in Spain for those over fourteen years of age was almost 53 percent. With only a gross figure of labor force participants, one can say little about the supply of labor in the market place. Its composition by age, sex, occupation, education level, and various other factors must be known to understand how the supply functions in the market.

The Labor Force

As indicated in chapter III, there has existed in Spain a concern about employment and the labor force for many years, but this interest has been in isolated government agencies with little power or authority to implement a coordinated or coherent manpower development program. And in many instances the concern with the labor force has been in global terms, rather than in the basic factor of education and skill levels and of occupations.

While a planning organization has existed in the Spanish government since the early 1960s, as late as 1969-1970 it has indicated little interest in developing a coordinated manpower program. The position taken by the Planning Commission[1] was that in Spain's stage of industrial development monetary, fiscal, and investment policies are the major factors of planning concern; and that only in economies much more highly developed than Spain's is there need for detailed planning of human resources. Such a conclusion is based on the hypothesis that in an economy where the level of development is low but starting to move upward rather rapidly there is no need to be concerned with the labor market. Because of the rapid growth of the economy, the supply of labor will be readily absorbed by the expanding economic sectors, regardless of the skills and training of the industrial labor force.

That such an unsophisticated view of economic growth and development may cause bottlenecks and distortions in many markets was not fully recognized by the Planning Commission although it was of some concern back in 1961 to a mission in Spain, organized by the International Bank for Reconstruction and Development. In its chapter on the industrial development of Spain, this report stated:[2]

> Greater flexibility and mobility of the labor force will help to increase its productivity. In addition there is need to raise the level of skills and productivity by more intensive vocational training. There are already shortages of some skills and more will become apparent as industrial growth proceeds unless the pace of vocational training is stepped up. As the demand for skilled labor at home increases, the emigration of trained personnel for employment elsewhere in Europe is less likely to continue, and this is desirable, since loss of such personnel in the future could handicap the growth of Spanish industry. The expansion of vocational training schools should be based on a careful study of requirements by industry, type of occupation and area. Special consideration should be given to the rapid retraining of workers who are seeking new employment after having been displaced.

This report also had noted that undue rigidity in the pattern of employment and compensation could impede the rationalization and growth of the industrial sector. By rigidity in employment patterns was meant the regulations regarding dismissals, since economic efficiency could conflict with the worker's interest in job security. By rigidity in compensation was meant the fifficulties to adapt the renumeration of employees to differences in, or to changes in, their productivity, especially at the plant level.[3]

While some ministries and departments have shown an interest and concern with these labor supply factors, the Planning Commission has mainly become involved in manpower at the global level, as the labor force interrelates with the indicative planning for the broadest economic sectors. Such a focus does have some value, as can be seen by table 10. From 1960 to 1968 the labor force engaged in agriculture and fishing has declined in both absolute and relative terms, while the industrial labor force has risen by about 15 percent and the labor force in services rose in excess of 20 percent. In 1960, agriculture represented over 41 percent of the labor force but by 1968 it had declined to 31 percent, and it was estimated that by 1971 it would drop to 25 percent. And while industry was substantially larger than services in 1960, the gap has been closing steadily over the years. Such shifts in growth patterns have their impact upon the composition of the labor force and the skills required. The education and skills needed in the agricultural sector are substantially different than those required for blue-collar jobs in the industrial sector or for white-collar jobs in the service sector.

TABLE 10

DISTRIBUTION OF THE LABOR FORCE BY
SECTORS, 1960-1968

| Year | Total Labor Force | | Agriculture and Fishing (Percent) | Industry (Percent) | Services (Percent) |
	Number (in thousands)	Percent			
1960	11,816.6	100.0	41.7	31.8	26.6
1961	11,839.3	100.0	40.0	32.6	27.4
1962	11,908.7	100.0	38.3	33.3	28.4
1963	11,988.7	100.0	36.6	34.0	29.4
1964	12,075.3	100.0	34.9	34.8	30.3
1965	12,176.9	100.0	33.2	35.5	31.3
1966	12,283.8	100.0	32.3	36.0	31.7
1967	12,404.6	100.0	31.7	36.1	32.1
1968	12,520.1	100.0	31.2	36.3	32.5
1971[1]	13,211.0	100.0	25.0	38.0	37.0

1. Estimate by Planning Commission.
Source: Computed from data of Instituto Nacional de Estadística, *Población activa en 1968*, (Madrid, 1969), p. XII.
Note: These figures on total labor force include estimates for the Spanish territories of Ceuta and Melilla, and for the military. Labor force figures in previous chapter were based on sample surveys, and did not include these two items.

Because of the nature of farm life and agricultural work, unemployment and underemployment are relatively common. With mechanization and more efficient use of farm land, the amount of surplus farm labor has grown rapidly, shifting many agricultural workers to the urban areas for industrial and service employment.

In 1966 the Ministry of Labor conducted a study of agricultural employment,[4] and it concluded that the agricultural labor force exceeded the demand

1. by some 700,000 persons, based on the 1966 levels of mechanization and structure;

mechanization of the agriculture sector (additional need of machinery in the magnitude of 300,000 tractors and 10,000 harvesters);

3. by approximately 1,800,000 persons, which would result if all farms were restructured to a minimum size considered technically adequate, and were mechanized accordingly (additional need of machinery in the magnitude of 600,000 tractors and 70,000 harvestors).[5]

While no land reform policy has been adopted in Spain, greater mechanization has occurred, with the resultant push of a growing number of agricultural workers off the land.

One may note that the labor force as a percentage of the total population[6] declined from 38.6 percent in 1960 to 38.2 percent in 1964 and to 37.8 percent in 1968. (See table 11.) Under conditions of an expanding economy one might normally expect that labor force as a percent of the total population would grow over time. One factor that may partly explain this phenomenon is the rather sharp growth, starting in the early 1960s, in the attendance of post-secondary schools, technical institutes, and universities. This could keep a significant number of young people (sixteen to twenty-four years of age) out of the labor force who would have entered at age sixteen. Another factor that may possibly explain the decline is the year after year net emigration of Spaniards which is probably not taken into account in estimating total population between decennial census years.

A more detailed description of the labor force is also given on table 11. While the labor force in agriculture declined by 20 percent over the period 1960-1968, mining declined even more, by nearly 32 percent. Commerce and other services showed the largest increases (49 percent and 32 percent respectively), while construction (28 percent) and manufacturing (23 percent) also showed rather substantial increases. Within the manufacturing group the largest rises occurred in durable goods industries such as transportation equipment (51 percent), and machinery, including electrical, (42 percent).

The distribution of labor force by major economic activity does not show any substantial changes over the eight-year period except the drop in agriculture from 42 percent to 31 percent. Mining as a percentage of total labor force also declined, but all other industries showed increases over the eight years.

It is interesting to note that in the year-to-year percentage changes for the total labor force, each successive year except 1968 showed larger increases. This pattern did not exist for any single major economic activity. However, both agriculture and mining showed declines in each year over the eight-year period, while all other industry groups showed increases in each year.

Unpublished materials of the Planning Commission present a forecast of the 1971 labor force, indicating a rise of 7.6 percent over 1965. This expected rate of increase is markedly higher than the 5.9 percent increase which occurred from 1960 to 1968.

TABLE 11

LABOR FORCE TREND BY ECONOMIC ACTIVITY,
FOR SELECTED YEARS
(in thousands)

Economic Activity	1960		1964		1968		Change 1960 to 1968	
	Number	Percent Distribution	Number	Percent Distribution	Number	Percent Distribution	Number	Percent
Agriculture and fishing	4,922.7	41.66	4,212.4	34.88	3,902.1	31.17	-1,020.6	-20.73
Mining	194.4	1.65	160.0	1.33	132.7	1.06	- 61.7	-31.74
Manufacturing	2,644.9	22.38	3,018.5	25.00	3,252.5	25.98	607.6	22.97
Food	395.4	3.34	431.3	3.57	460.8	3.68	65.4	16.94
Textiles	596.6	5.04	660.5	5.46	690.9	5.51	94.3	15.81
Paper	111.1	0.94	130.3	1.07	143.9	1.14	32.8	29.52
Chemicals	174.6	1.47	193.8	1.60	221.2	1.76	46.6	26.69
Glass & ceramics	150.0	1.26	172.4	1.42	187.1	1.49	37.1	24.73
Metal (exc. machinery)	417.3	3.53	481.5	3.98	529.5	4.22	112.2	26.89
Machinery (incl. elec.)	185.7	1.57	234.1	1.93	263.5	2.10	77.8	41.90
Transportation equipment	216.1	1.82	284.7	2.35	326.5	2.60	110.4	51.09
All other	398.1	3.36	429.9	3.56	429.1	3.42	31.0	7.79
Construction	837.1	7.09	936.4	7.76	1,074.2	8.58	237.1	28.32
Electricity, water & gas	80.2	0.68	83.8	0.69	89.1	0.71	8.9	11.10
Commerce	865.3	8.17	1,121.9	9.29	1,286.5	10.28	421.2	48.68
Transportation & communication	546.4	4.62	583.4	4.83	632.8	5.05	86.4	15.81
Other services	1,625.6	13.75	1,958.9	16.22	2,150.2	17.17	524.6	32.27
TOTAL	11,816.6	100.00	12,075.3	100.00	12,520.1	100.00	703.5	5.95
Labor Force as Percent of Total Population	38.58%	—	38.21%	—	37.85%	—	—	—

Source: Instituto Nacional de Estadística, Población activa en 1968 (Madrid, 1969), pp. XII and XV.

A forecast of the 1971 labor force, by level of training, is shown in table 12. Here one sees that unskilled workers in the labor force have declined since 1965, and the forecast for 1971 shows a drop of 26 percent. Over the six-year period the number of administrators was expected to drop slightly by 1.2 percent, and the number of semiskilled workers was expected to increase slightly, by 0.2 percent. The largest expected increases were for high-level and medium-level white-collar employees (about 40 percent), while most other groups showed expected increases of about 35 percent. It appears that supply is expected to adjust to the rather sharp drop in the demand for unskilled workers and to the leveling off of the demand for semiskilled workers. These data point up the necessity of increases in enrollments at the university and in the vocational training programs in order to have a supply of labor with a closer approximation of skills and occupations required by the employing units in the labor market.

A distribution of the labor force by socioeconomic groups and by cultural levels indicates a rather wide spread in the percentage of illiterates. (See appendix table IV-1.) Of the 12.3 million persons in the labor force, approximately 511,000, or 4.2 percent were illiterates. There was no illiteracy within employer groups, professionals, managers, and high-level employees. However, illiteracy rates were rather high for farm laborers (15.1 percent), service workers (8.8 percent), and unskilled workers (6.4 percent). In relatively few socioeconomic groups did a majority complete their special studies. Of the professionals, high-level employees, and managers of firms, only the first two had a majority complete their studies with a university degree.

The percentage of female illiterates in the labor force exceeded that of the male illiterates by less than two percentage points (5.6 percent compared to 3.7 percent). While the males showed a larger percent of university graduates, the females had a larger percent of secondary school degree holders. If these two educational levels were combined, the percentage of males and of females would differ by only 0.18 percent.

In 1960, female workers were about 18 percent of the labor force, and by 1968 the ratio had increased to 24 percent, quite a substantial gain. However, the participation of females in the Spanish labor force is still relatively low, while in the United States, for example, females in 1968 represented 37 percent of the total labor force. As shown in appendix table IV-2, the ratio of females in the Spanish labor force of those under twenty-five years of age is 30 percent or over, while the ratio in the prime working years twenty-five to sixty-four was under 20 percent. The pattern of married females returning to the labor force, or entering it for the first time, after their children have grown up, has not yet developed. The social custom of women not working outside the home has only recently been breached on a relatively large scale, and principally by the younger women. It may take considerably more time before it is

socially accepted for all women to enter the labor force. Looking at the
same data in a different perspective, one notes that of all the women in
the labor force about 37 percent are under twenty-five years of age, and
30 percent are between twenty-five and forty-four years old, in con-
trast to the comparable male figures of 20 percent and 39 percent,
respectively. In general, the females in the labor force are younger
than the males.

The Unemployment Situation

One significant measure of how closely the labor supply meets the
manpower requirements is unemployment. The existence of unemployment is not a measure of the overabundance of the supply any more than
it is a measure of the shortage of the demand for labor. What unemployment does indicate is the degree to which the labor market fails to
adjust the supply and demand, given the various wage rates in the
market. From a purely expository position, unemployment may be considered a measure of an unused part of the labor force.

TABLE 12

LABOR FORCE IN SPAIN BY LEVEL OF TRAINING,[1]
1965, 1966, 1967 AND FORECAST FOR 1971
(in thousands)

Level of Training	1965	1966	1967	1971 Forecast	Difference 1965 to 1971 Absolute	Percent
Administrators	72.6	71.4	70.8	71.4	-1.2	-1.65
Professionals	162.7	172.4	182.3	217.9	55.2	33.93
Technicians	370.1	388.7	407.9	475.3	105.2	28.42
High-level white-collar employees	119.7	129.1	138.4	169.7	50.0	41.77
Medium-level white-collar employees	486.3	520.6	555.5	681.5	195.2	40.14
White-collar employees	822.3	874.1	926.9	1,113.6	291.3	35.43
Foremen and Superintendents	783.6	838.6	892.4	1,062.9	279.3	35.64
Skilled workers	2,728.0	2,883.5	3,044.4	3,631.3	903.3	33.11
Semiskilled workers	3,139.0	3,154.7	3,172.2	3,145.1	6.1	0.19
Unskilled workers	3,590.5	3,369.6	3,181.5	2,641.9	-948.6	-26.42
TOTAL	12,274.8	12,402.7	12,572.3	13,210.6	935.8	7.62

[1] Level of training is a translation of phrase "Viveles de Formación."
Source: Unpublished data obtained from Planning Commission, but statistics are from Ministry of Labor.

Despite evidence to the contrary, the official position of the government is that the unemployment rate is very low. As shown on table 13,
one set of government statistics shows the unemployment rate con-

sistently under 2 percent since 1960. There are various official unemployment estimates, all based principally upon the number of unemployed persons who register for jobs at the relatively few employment offices in the large urban areas. All these estimates show unemployment rates below 2 percent. (See table 14.)

In a special nongovernment survey in 1969[7] unemployment statistics were collected for Madrid, and the rate was considerably higher than the government figures. The unemployment rate for white-collar workers was 2 percent, but the rate for blue-collar workers rose from 2 percent in 1966 to 6 percent in 1969. In this latter year, the unemployment rate was 9 percent for unskilled workers and 4 percent for skilled workers.

In general, Madrid is considered an area of relatively low unemployment. Looking at registered unemployment, where statistics are available by province, Madrid unemployment rate is below the national average, and significantly below such provinces as Cádiz, Córdoba, Jaén, Málaga, and Sevilla. If the FOESSA estimate of unemployment in Madrid is valid, it is likely that the national average is considerably above 6 percent, a rather unsatisfactory situation. There is, however, no valid method of determining how far off the published unemployment statistics are from reality. It should also be noted that substantial emigration of Spanish workers to various western European countries has relieved the unemployment situation in Spain. If the net number of emigrants over the past 10 years were added to the official number of unemployed, the unemployment rate would triple, from 1.9 percent to 6.2 percent.[8]

Using INE statistics, table 15 shows the number of unemployed and the unemployment rate by economic activity for 1960 and 1968. Because many of the unemployed farm workers seek work in the nonagricultural sectors, and because the large amount of underemployment is not included in the unemployment count, the unemployment rate in agriculture is below the national average. Mining had a slightly above-average unemployment rate in 1960, but by 1968 the rate had jumped to 6.5 percent (from 1.8 percent in 1960), the highest rate for all industries. The second highest rate in 1968 was construction, with 5.3 percent unemployment; in 1960 it had been highest with an unemployment rate of 4.8 percent. Within the manufacturing group enemployment in 1968 ranged from a low of 0.4 percent in transportation equipment to a high of 4.8 percent in textiles. There seems to be little pattern between the two years presented.

According to the National Institute of Statistics, about 22 percent of the unemployed could be considered as long-term unemployed, that is, unemployed for at least six months, while about 27 percent were unemployed less than one month. Males, representing about 88 percent of the unemployed, naturally showed a similar pattern in duration of unemployment. Approximately 13 percent of the total number unemployed were seeking their first job, and of these about 30 percent were long-term unemployed and another 30 percent were unemployed less than one month.

About 80 percent of all those seeking work in Spain in 1968 were unemployed, and the remaining 20 percent were employed but seeking work. Of the latter, about one-third were unskilled workers and another third were skilled. Of the unemployed, about 54 percent were unskilled and about one-quarter were skilled. The male unemployed showed a similar distribution, but of the female unemployed 45 percent were unskilled, 17 percent were skilled workers and 30 percent were office and other white-collar workers.

TABLE 13

TREND OF UNEMPLOYMENT, 1960-1968
(in thousands)

Year	Labor Force	Number of Unemployed	Unemployment Rate
1960	11,816.6	175.7	1.49
1961	11,839.3	173.7	1.47
1962	11,908.7	142.4	1.20
1963	11,988.7	160.3	1.34
1964	12,075.3	184.3	1.53
1965	12,176.9	183.0	1.50
1966	12,283.8	165.8	1.35
1967	12,404.6	231.1	1.86
1968	12,520.1	240.1	1.92

Source: Instituto Nacional de Estadística, *Población activa en 1968* (Madrid, 1969), pp. XII and XIII.

TABLE 14

COMPARISON OF UNEMPLOYMENT ESTIMATES
FOR VARIOUS YEARS

Unemployment Estimates	1964	1965	1967	1968
Registered Unemployment (Official)	129,644[1]	147.043[2]	147,341[3]	182,016[3]
Estimated (Ministry of Labor)	153,967[1]	188,146[2]	187,447[5]	246,050[5]
Percent over Registered	18.7%	28.0%	27.2%	35.2%
Estimated (National Statistics Office)	184,300[4]	183,000[4]	231,100[4]	240,100[4]
Percent over Registered	42.2%	24.4%	56.7%	31.9%

Sources:
1. Ministerio de Trabajo, *Dinámica del empleo en 1964* (Madrid, 1965), pp. 89-93.
2. Ministerio de Trabajo, *Dinámica del empleo en 1965* (Madrid, 1966), p. 197.
3. Organización Sindical, Vicesecretario Nacional de Ordenación Económica, *Evolución socioeconómica de España 1968* (Madrid, 1969), p. 50.
4. Instituto Nacional de Estadística, *Población activa en 1968* (Madrid, 1969), p. XIII.
5. Cited in Fundación FOESSA, *op. cit.*, p. 1073, as figures from Ministry of Labor.

TABLE 15

LABOR FORCE AND UNEMPLOYMENT, BY ECONOMIC
ACTIVITY 1960 AND 1968
(in thousands)

Economic Activity	1960			1968		
	Labor Force	Number of unemployed	Rate of unemployed	Labor Force	Number of unemployed	Rate of unemployed
Agriculture & fishing	4,922.7	66.9	1.36%	3,902.1	52.2	1.34%
Mining	194.4	3.5	1.80	132.7	8.6	6.48
Manufacturing	2,644.9	38.2	1.44	3,252.5	79.8	2.45
Food	395.4	8.2	2.07	460.8	10.0	2.17
Textiles	596.6	11.0	1.84	690.9	33.1	4.79
Paper	111.1	1.3	1.17	143.9	2.6	1.81
Chemicals	174.6	3.8	2.18	221.2	3.4	1.54
Glass & ceramics	150.0	0.5	0.33	187.1	1.1	0.59
Metal (excl. machinery)	417.3	3.4	0.81	529.5	15.2	2.87
Machinery (incl. elec.)	185.7	2.2	1.18	263.5	5.9	2.24
Transportation equip.	216.1	1.0	0.46	326.5	1.3	0.40
All other	398.1	6.8	1.71	429.1	7.2	1.68
Construction	837.1	40.1	4.79	1,074.2	57.3	5.33
Electricity, water, gas	80.2	3.4	4.24	89.1	0.9	1.01
Commerce	865.3	6.4	0.74	1,286.5	7.0	0.54
Transportation & communication	546.4	4.0	0.73	632.8	8.5	1.34
TOTAL	11,816.6	175.7	1.49	12,520.1	240.1	1.92

Source: Instituto Nacional de Estadística, *Población activa en 1968* (Madrid, 1969), pp. XII and XIII.

Migration and the Labor Force

Emigration can be an important outlet for surplus manpower in the labor force. In a situation where unemployment is substantial, or may be growing, there is always some pressure on the unemployed to leave the country and seek employment elsewhere. Under certain circumstances even the employed may be enticed to migrate by the lure of greater economic gains in the host country. It is obvious that at all times emigration is dependent on the economic conditions in the host countries.

For many years many Spaniards migrated across the Atlantic to Latin American countries, and starting in 1959 there began a migration to Western European Countries which made a real impact on reducing unemployment in the nation. As indicated in an ILO report,

. . . credit for the unemployment figures recorded (in Spain) cannot be given entirely to the propitious aspects of the economic situation since they are also partly due to emigration to various countries in Western Europe (Federal Republic of Germany,

France and Switzerland), which has helped to stabilize the employment market.[9]

The collection and publication of statistics on emigration seem to be a rather haphazard affair. Tables 16 and 17 present what hopefully are the basic data on emigration, but there are doubts. Table 16 refers to permanent migrants to continental Europe, but the reference to "permanent" is based on an inference. Most sources for these statistics make no reference other than that the figures are for emigrants to continental Europe, but one source with almost identical figures also contained statistics for seasonal emigrants which far exceeded the figures for "continental" emigrants.[10] While most sources are silent on who the emigrants are, one source states that these figures refer to members of the labor force (while the data on emigrants to countries across the Atlantic refer to total population).[11] The data in table 17 also refer to migrants who are permanent residents, and again this assumption is based on an inference. While the numerous official documents quote these statistics, only one[12] indicates that the figures refer to total population, and shows the data by age group and sex. The statistics on this table are quoted in numerous government and nongovernment reports, and are referred to as Spanish emigrants across the sea (emigracion Espanola a ultramar). One would assume that these figures are totals of all those migrating across the sea, but one source[13] presents these statistics as emigration by ship, and then presents a second series of annual statistics of emigrants by air, which would increase the numbers in the original series by 25 to 50 percent.

Despite these difficulties with the emigration figures, some analysis of the effects of migration on the labor market is warranted. As indicated in table 16, the year-by-year movement of Spanish emigrants to European countries as permanent residents was not large, relative to the size of the labor force. Even in the peak years of 1962-1966, no single year total of emigrants exceeded 1.6 percent of the labor force. And while these Spaniards were emigrating, many others were returning home. The largest net outflow took place in 1961 with a figure of 108,200, while it is estimated that in 1967 there was a net return to Spain of 25,000. Taking the net figure for each year as a percent of the labor force in that year shows less than a 1 percent effect in any one year. However, if this net outflow were considered as part of the unemployed labor force, the unemployment rate would have been from 50 percent to 100 percent larger than the government indicated.

However, the cumulative effect over time of the net emigration to continental Europe may have had a very strong impact on the labor market. Totaling the net emigration for the nine years, 1959-1967, one finds that there was a loss to the labor force of 420,267 persons, or about 3.4 percent. If all these emigrants living in western Europe in 1967 returned to Spain and did not find employment, the unemployment rate would have nearly tripled, from 1.9 percent to 5.3 percent. This is significant. From another source[14] figures for 1968 were 123,800 departers for Europe and 74,400 returns, for a net emigration of 49,400; and for 1969, 165,300 departures and 95,600 returns for a net emigration of 69,700. If these figures are added to the possible total of unemployed, the unemployment rate would rise to 6.2 percent.

TABLE 16

SPANISH EMIGRATION TO EUROPE (PERMANENT
RESIDENTS) 1959-1967

Year	Number of Emigrants	Number of Returnees	Net Emigrants	Net Emigrants As Percent of Labor Force	Net Emigrants Plus Unemployed as Percent of Labor Force
1959	20,580	22,209	-1,629	-0.01	—
1960	40,189	12,194	27,995	0.23	1.72
1961	116,524	8,315	108,209	0.91	2.38
1962	147,692	46,344	101,348	0.85	2.05
1963	147,859	52,730	93,129	0.78	2.12
1964	192,999	98,993	83,818	0.69	2.22
1965	181,279	120,678	60,600	0.50	2.00
1966	141,997	143,082	-1,085	-0.01	1.34
1967	60,000	85,000	-25,000	-0.20	1.46

Source: Data for years 1959-1966 from Comisaría del Plan de Desarrollo Económico y Social, Ponencia de Trabajo de II Plan, unpublished report, p. 20; for the year 1967 figures are estimates taken from Comisaría del Plan de Desarrollo Económico y Social, Factores humanos y sociales (Madrid, 1967), p. 33.

Table 17 shows the year-to-year emigration across the Atlantic and the returns, for 1959-1967. The number of overseas emigrants was nowhere as large as that leaving for European countries, and the number of returnees has been exceeding the emigrants each year beginning with 1964. The net number of emigrants as a percent of the labor force never attained 0.15 percent in any one year.[15] Two problems must be handled before one can cumulate the figures on overseas emigrants to determine the total impact on the labor force. One must first estimate what proportion would have been in the labor force, and then determine how far back the statistics should be cumulated to determine a realistic impact on the labor force.

In a report by the Ministry of Labor in 1964 both these problems were examined and handled in the following manner:[16] (1) after analyzing the age distribution of the emigrants and returnees and the general rates of participation in the labor force, a participation rate of 53 percent was computed and applied to emigrants and a 58 percent rate to the returnees; and (2) figures going back to 1950 were used, as a minimum amount that could have affected the labor force.[17]

Using this procedure we cumulated the overseas emigration statistics for the period 1950-1967, and applied the 53 percent participation rate to the emigrants and the 58 percent to the returnees. This gave us 377,342 labor force emigrants and 188,114 returnees, for a net loss of 189,228, or about 1.5 percent of the labor force. If this were added to the cumulative net figure for emigrants to other European countries, the total would be 4.9 percent of the labor force, or 5.8 percent if 1968 and 1969 data on net European migration were included. If all these persons returned to Spain (or had not left Spain) and did not find employment, this would increase the official 1.9 percent unemployment rate to a total of 6.8 percent, or 7.7 percent if 1968 and 1969 data were included.

TABLE 17

SPANISH EMIGRATION TO COUNTRIES
ACROSS THE ATLANTIC (PERMANENT RESIDENTS) 1959-1968

Year	Number of Emigrants	Number of Returnees	Net Emigrants	Net as Percent of Labor Force
1959	34,550	19,100	15,450	0.13
1960	33,242	23,114	10,128	0.09
1961	34,370	24,197	10,173	0.09
1962	32,295	22,321	9,974	0.08
1963	23,024	22,322	702	0.01
1964	21,067	22,434	-1,367	-0.01
1965	16,855	21,192	-4,337	-0.04
1966	16,079	20,081	-4,002	-0.03
1967	13,867	18,597	-4,730	-0.04
1968	13,674	—	—	—

Source: Data for years 1959-1966 from Comisaria del Plan de Desarrollo Económico y Social, Ponencia de Trabajo de II Plan, unpublished report, p. 19; data for 1967 from Comisaría del Plan de Desarrollo Económico y Social, *Factores humanos y sociales* (Madrid 1967), p. 33; figure for 1968 from Instituto Nacional de Estadística, *Anuario Estadístico de España*, 1970, edicion manual (Madrid, 1970) p. 53.

How one should treat seasonal emigrants, from the point of view of Spanish labor markets, is not a simple problem. During the years 1964-1967 an average of approximately 100,000 workers per year left Spain for varying periods of time to harvest crops in other countries. There is no information on whether these seasonal workers are generally unemployed or would have been unemployed had they remained at home. It is very likely, however, that these workers would have been unemployed or underemployed during some part of the time they worked abroad. At a maximum this would add about 0.75 percent to the unemployment rate in any year.

One additional factor in Spanish emigration is the Intergovernmental Committee for European Migration, (ICEM), an international organization whose principal function is to help move European refugees to other parts of the world. With a decline in the refugee problem the organization assumed the additional function of assisting selective migration to less developed countries where certain skills and occupations were needed. ICEM has an office in Spain, and over the years it has helped a few thousand Spaniards with professional and technical skills, as well as skilled craftsmen, emigrate to Latin American countries and to Australia, where specific jobs at predetermined wages awaited them. The number of such Spanish emigrants aided by ICEM has been relatively small, with about 700 in 1967, and 1,000 in 1968, some of whom undoubtedly were family members, not part of the labor force. While many of the emigrants were persons with high skills, the total numbers involved are too small to have had a measurable impact on the labor force. Their reasons for emigrating generally included a view that opportunities would be greater overseas.

Perhaps more than offsetting this selected emigration is the number of foreigners who are residents in Spain. In recent years the number has been increasing at about 10 percent a year; in 1968 foreign residents totaled 127,000, or about one percent of the labor force.[18]

Overall, these seem to be sufficient evidence that the net emigration has relieved the pressure on the labor market by reducing significantly the potential unemployment situation. As indicated above, the emigration had the effect of reducing the unemployment rate for 1967 from something in excess of 7 percent to the officially cited figure of 1.9 percent.

A substantial number of the emigrants were workers from the agricultural sector of the economy which had a tremendous surplus of workers;[19] and many other emigrants were unskilled and semiskilled industrial workers for whom job and earning opportunities were small and economic advancement possibilities were limited. Thus, there was an obvious advantage for Spain's economy, and this was coupled with the significant amount of foreign exchange that was sent back to Spain by these emigrants. Such remittances ran close to 350 million dollars a year during the period 1962-1967.[20] A third advantage to the large numbers of emigrants was that many of the returnees had gained experience as industrial workers in some of the more modern plants and industries in Western Europe; and others had received on-the-job training for a wide range of jobs in modern industry. In many cases this type of experience and training could not have been provided in Spain, but even if it were available it was provided to Spain at zero cost.

This seems to be an example of the classic case of industrialized nations helping train the workers of the less developed countries. And in the classic case these newly trained workers become the core of experienced industrial workers in their own country, and help train their fellow countrymen. Undoubtedly some of this occurred, but it was the general impression within the government and the private sector[21] that the experience and training gained abroad was frequently not applicable or that these returnees could not find employment where their newly acquired skills would be used. In any event, many of the returnees used their accumulated savings to open small retail and service shops, and they have become a part of the growing number in the lower middle class.

Sources of Trained Manpower

While the basic source of the supply of labor is the population, what interests us most is manpower that makes itself available on the labor market with skills that are needed or can be used by the employers of labor. Despite obligatory schooling through age thirteen, youngsters below this age and with little or no skills to offer enter the labor market and seek jobs. Such youths are not necessarily condemned to a life of unskilled work; there are ways outside the formal education and training system for persons to acquire skills. Many private firms conduct formal or informal on-the-job training programs for employees who show promise, and unknown numbers of workers acquire skills in this manner. In addition some workers pick up various skills by observing other workers perform. There are no statistics on persons who acquire their skills in these manners, and therefore there is no way of planning for their "output." The only way to further such noninstitutional training is to develop financial or other incentives for employers to start such on-the-job training programs in their own plants.

Spain has had a system of education and training for many years but only in the past five years has the rate of growth of school attendance increased substantially. There has been greater concern about the structure of its educational system since the beginning of its Plan I in 1964, and in 1969 the Ministry of Education issued a report on the educational system including proposals for improving and expanding the whole structure.[22] Despite some recent gains, Spain is still considerably behind most other European countries as measured by various indicators of education standards. One measure is public expenditure on education as a percentage of national income, and Spain was low with a rate of 1.5 percent, compared to 4.2 percent in Germany, 7.1 percent in Belgium, 4.6 percent in France, 2.3 percent in Greece, and 4.6 percent in Switzerland.[23]

Another measure of the school system is the rate of school attendance by age, and here again Spain does not show up well in comparison with other Western European countries.[24] In 1966, school attendance in Spain was 86 percent for the six- to nine-year old age group; 60 percent for the ten- to sixteen-year old age group; and 9 percent for the seventeen- to twenty-four-year old age group. Comparable rates for France were 100 percent, 83 percent, and 17 percent. Comparing the trends of school attendance in a few countries, one study concludes that by this criterion, Spain is about fifteen years behind France and about five years behind Italy.[25] Focusing on higher education, Spain is behind other countries in a comparison of average number of registered students per 100,000 population.[26] In 1964, Spain's figure was 355 compared to 512 in Italy, 648 in Greece, and 940 in France.

These various comparisons are not much more than indications of the level of Spain's educational system and its potential for improvement. At this point, we are interested principally in the country's ability to produce trained and skilled manpower,[27] and the evidence seems to show that it has considerable leeway for improvement if only to catch up with its European neighbors. We can here examine briefly the mechanisms which annually feed numbers of person into the labor force, and the gross amounts that are turned out regularly.

Of the 5.5 million persons in the school system only a small percent are being trained or educated for a specific task or area of work that would put the person above the unskilled level on the labor market. If enrollments of the primary and secondary schools are excluded, this would leave less than 500,000 whose education offers them the opportunity of acquiring some marketable skills. One can readily question the merit, from the point of view of the labor market, of this distribution of enrollments (and also of the public expenditures).

One cannot assume that all of those currently enrolled in the different programs will complete the required years of study. Many will drop out of school before completion and then enter the labor market. There is no information on the type of job such dropouts obtain, but institutional and cultural factors would lead us to assume that failure to obtain the diploma, certificate, degree, or license given when a program is completed would preclude the dropout from many job opportunities. The title that comes with a completed program normally is the minimum requirement for many entry-point jobs above the unskilled level.

A significant number of students are enrolled in programs for the training of craftsmen and technicians. The largest numbers are involved in vocational training programs, especially for industrial work (approximately 126,000). At the technician level, one would aggregate the 69,000 in the intermediate level technical schools, the 7,000 sanitation technical assistants, and the 55,000 in the technical secondary schools. All told, approximately 260,000 youths are being trained directly or indirectly for craftsman and technical jobs large in an absolute sense, but relatively small compared to the 930,000 in the liberal arts university-preparatory secondary schools.

One interesting aspect of the sources of the labor supply is vocational training of adults. Such training generally is for adults already in the labor force, either as unskilled workers or as workers with obsolete skills, and therefore does not contribute to a net additional of numbers to the labor force. However, if through such training a worker's productivity is significantly higher, the labor supply is markedly different than before. Through various government agencies and the Sindicato Organization, numerous adult training programs have been developed around the country. Private correspondence courses have also expanded. It is estimated that the number of adults receiving training in these programs has increased from 74,000 in 1964 to 177,700 in 1967,[28] more than doubling over a three-year period. However, in view of the number of unskilled agricultural workers who are shifting to the industrial sector of the economy, vocational training for adults will have to expand much more if it is to make a dent in the surplus of farm labor.

There is considerable awareness in Spain of the weaknesses of its ed-

ucational and training system. The Ministry of Education's White
Book proposed a relatively comprehensive reorganization of the system
and increased opportunites for the lower income group to participate
in the improved programs. The Planning Commission has proposed
more schools, increased financial aid to students, a high priority on
vocational training, improved quality of education, and improved research capability. One estimate[29] sees enrollments of higher education doubling between 1968 and 1975. There undoubtedly will be
changes in the educational system, but there seems to be little concern,
at the higher levels of the government, about its impact on the labor
market.

In a global sense the sources of labor supply—the educational and
training systems in the country—can turn out sufficient numbers of
persons with some skills. However, whether these new recruits to the
labor force will be in the right geographic location, in the right industry with the right skills, is questionable. The following two chapters
(V and VI) discuss the processes of human capital formation, with
special details on the system of higher education. Chapter VII then
attempts to analyze the processes of manpower allocation.

V

THE PROCESSES
OF HUMAN CAPITAL FORMATION

The formation of human capital is a multifacet process including both formal and informal methods. The informal means of development include all kinds of on-the-job training and experience, as well as a wide range of other personal experiences that improve human capital or make it more valuable. In view of the informality, there are no guidelines or structures to these means of human capital formation, nor are there data on how many persons in specified occupations have acquired their skills through such means. We do know, however, that substantial numbers of persons must acquire their skills in informal ways, because far less than 100 percent of the labor force have completed a formal training program. Despite the numbers that are probably involved in informal training, decisions on such training are being made by thousands of individual firms whose prime interest in the training is to meet their own needs for specialized manpower. A central authority such as the government has little control over the decisions on such training, and therefore the government cannot base any education and training plans for the country on the informal means of human capital formation.

The formal education and training system in Spain is run or directed principally by the government. Where private organizations are permitted to operate, the government has prescribed rules and regulations to assure the population of a somewhat equal treatment with those who enter the government system. It is this formal system, both public and private, that the government can manipulate and adjust to strive for the goals it establishes with reference to human capital formation.

The Formal Educational System
Primary school education (and perhaps even pre-primary education) is a prerequisite for the more advanced specialized education programs

that prepare students with particular marketable skills. Whether primary education is investment or consumption is a moot point. For those persons who continue on in the educational system, elementary school would have to be considered as investment in human capital. For the many who do not go beyond primary education, this can be considered either investment or consumption.

While our interest is in the process of human capital formation, primary education is obligatory in Spain for all, and regardless of the personal reasons for attendance it must be considered as a basic part of investment in human capital. We may note that there are many persons enrolled in various educational programs beyond primary education who are involved because of cultural, social, or esthetic reasons. How many persons are so involved cannot be determined and we must therefore examine the whole educational system and structure as if it contributed entirely to the process of human capital formation.

One of the simplest measures of the educational system of a country is its literacy rate. The elimination of illiteracy is a common goal of countries around the world, and the speed with which a country approaches this goal is one measure of quality of the educational system. At the turn of the century illiteracy in Spain was high, at 56 percent of the population. However, illiteracy declined steadily in each subsequent decade, with the sharpest drops occurring in the 1920s (10.9 percent decline) and in the 1930s (9.3 percent decline). In 1960, illiteracy was only 12.1 percent and it is estimated that illiteracy has fallen significantly since then.[1]

From 1963 to 1968, Spain developed a special campaign to wipe out illiteracy, and by the end of 1967, the illiteracy rate was 5.7 percent of the population aged fifteen and over, and 3 percent of the population between fifteen and sixty years of age. There were thus about 640,000 illiterate persons in Spain, ranging from a low of about 0.1 percent in the Province of Baleares to 12.7 percent in the Province of Cadiz. The illiteracy rate in Madrid Province was 1.3 percent.[2]

Looking at the adult population of sixteen years of age and over in 1960 (the latest year for which census data are available), one notes that about 94 percent had no more than primary school education, which at that time was a six-year program.[3] (See table 18.) Thus, many of these may have had less than six years of schooling, but no statistics on this are available. Almost 4 percent of the adult population had attended secondary school, and only 1 percent higher education. In 1960, the average educational level of the Spanish adults would have to be considered relatively low.

By various yardsticks, Spain's level of education in 1966 was not as high as that of other Western European countries in 1964. (See appendix table V-1.) Spain had 171 students per 1000 population, while Italy had 177 and France 224. In the distribution of student enrollment by level of education, Spain showed the highest percent in the primary

TABLE 18

CLASSIFICATION OF SPANISH POPULATION OVER FIFTEEN YEARS OF AGE ACCORDING TO SCHOOLS ATTENDED
(1960 Census)

	Total	Primary[1]	Vocational Training	Secondary				Higher Education	Information Not Recorded
				Total	General	Vocational	Technical		
Male	10,005,801	9,196,894	69,988	465,759	278,978	76,533	110,248	199,247	73,913
Female	9,876,494	9,434,865	20,671	282,366	148,080	105,706	28,580	18,671	119,921
Total	19,882,295	18,631,759	90,659	748,125	427,058	182,239	138,828	217,918	193,834
Percent	100.0	93.7	0.4	3.8	2.1	0.9	0.7	1.1	1.0

1. There are no data on the number of years they attended school.
Source: Instituto Nacional de Estadística, as quoted in Ministerio de Educación y Ciencia, *Datos y cifras de la enseñanza en España, 1969,* Tomo 1, estadísticos (Madrid, 1969), p. 18.

level. Expenditures in education is another index of a country's concern
with education and of the quality of education. Compared with a number of European countries, Spain's public expenditure on education as
a percent of gross national product and of total public expenditure was
relatively low, as shown in appendix table V-2. In the former measure,
Spain showed 1.8 percent, compared with 4.8 percent in Italy, 4.4 percent in France, and 3.6 percent in Germany. In the latter measure,
Germany was lowest with 10.9 percent; however, Spain's 11.7 percent
was considerably smaller than the 19.8 percent rate in Italy and the 19.1
percent in France.

In terms of the relevant age groups, from age two through age thirty,
school enrollment as a percent of the population was 36.3 percent in
Spain compared to 51.4 percent in France, a rather substantial difference. (See table 19.) In the primary school age groups, the difference in
enrollment rates between the two countries was not too great, but in the
secondary school age groups the enrollment rates in Spain were less
than half those in France. At the higher ages, again the differences between the two countries were not substantial. Disregarding the' pre-
primary age group, the critical age in school attendance seems to be at
fourteen, where the rate of attendance was 39.7 percent, a very sharp
drop from the 67.2 percent attendance rate at age thirteen. In view of
the obligatory school attendance through age thirteen in Spain, the
sharp drop in attendance rate at age fourteen is not completely unexpected.

In primary education there is a higher rate of enrollment at age six
than at the age of seven, eight, or nine, which may be owing to classrooms created by new construction are usually for those six-year olds
who are beginning obligatory education.[4] The implication of this is
that the depressed enrollment rates for the seven-, eight-, and nine-year
olds result in part from the lack of classrooms. The enrollment rates are
very high at ages ten and eleven because of double enrollment in certain
sectors of the school population, especially rural, at these ages. An unknown number of students are enrolled in primary school, and at the
same time they are enrolled for the baccalaureate degree through what
is called "free" education.[5] Students will engage in this double enrollment because without actual attendance at a secondary school they may
make sufficient progress toward the bachelor's degree that would
permit them to matriculate in the university.

The sharp drops in school enrollments at certain ages may also reflect
the difficulties imposed by certain examinations in the educational
system. For example, in the academic year 1965-1966, less than 50 percent of the students enrolled passed the examination for the lower
baccalaureate degree, and the preuniversity examination[6] was passed by
only 42.6 percent. Indicative of these dropout points, it is interesting to
note that of every 100 students who began primary education in 1951,
27 entered secondary school, 18 passed the lower baccalaureate exam,

TABLE 19

PERCENTAGE OF POPULATION ATTENDING
SCHOOL, BY AGE, SPAIN AND FRANCE, 1966

Years of Age	Spain	France	Normal Level of Education
2 years old	1.8	11.4	
3	9.6	45.0	Pre-primary
4	40.8	75.0	
5	57.5	98.5	
6	91.5	100.0	
7	87.4	100.0	
8	86.0	100.0	
9	84.7	100.0	Primary
10	93.8	100.0	
11	92.4	100.0	
12	85.7	100.0	
13	67.2	98.3	
14	39.7	74.2	
15	27.6	59.9	Secondary
16	20.6	52.1	
17	17.7	38.0	
18	14.0	26.2	
19	12.8	18.2	
20	11.0	11.6	
21	6.6	9.8	Higher
22	5.8	6.3	
23	4.8	5.1	
24	4.6	3.9	
25-30	1.6	2.3	
TOTAL	36.3	51.4	

Source: Comisaría Plan, *Enseñanza y formación profesional* (Madrid, 1967), p. 22.
Fundación FOESSA, *op cit.*, p. 954.

10 passed the higher baccalaureate, 5 passed the preuniversity exam, and 3 finished their university studies in 1967.[7]

Of the total number of students in the whole educational system in the academic year 1967-1968, over 60 percent were in primary schools and an additional 10 percent were in pre-primary schools. About 24 percent were enrolled in secondary school programs, and of these 19 percent were in general baccalaureate programs and 1 percent in technical baccalaureate programs. Less than 2.4 percent were registered in vocational training programs, and about 2.3 percent were enrolled in intermediate programs most of which were in normal schools. Only 2.6 percent of all the student in the educational system were studying at institutions of higher education. (See table 20.)

TABLE 20

NUMBER OF STUDENTS IN THE EDUCATIONAL SYSTEM, BY LEVEL OF
EDUCATION 1966-1967 AND 1967-68

Level of Education	1966-67	1967-68	Percent Change	Percent Distribution, 1967-68
Preprimary	603,786	626,293	3.7	10.7
Primary	3,421,458	3,552,393	3.8	60.5
Secondary				
General baccalaureate[1]	929,589	1,119,803	20.5	19.1
Technical baccalaureate[1]	55,221	61,946	12.1	1.0
Vocational training-industrial	132,394	135,942	2.7	2.3
Vocational training-nautical	2,231	2,517	12.8	0.04
Commerce	21,911	24,280	10.8	0.4
Art	45,509	44,628	-2.0	0.8
Assistant health technician	7,060	8,625	22.2	0.1
Intermediate				
Normal school	68,972	69,110	0.2	1.2
Intermediate technical	64,556	65,380	1.3	1.1
Nautical	2,340	2,708	15.7	0.04
Higher Education				
University	105,370	116,440	10.5	2.0
Technical	36,038	38,692	7.4	0.6
Art	2,745	3,221	17.3	0.05
TOTAL	5,499,180	5,871,978	6.8	100.0

1. The bachelor's degree is granted after completion of spefcified programs at the secondary school level.
Source: Ministerio de Educación y Ciencia, *Datos y cifras de la enseñanza en España 1969*, Tomo 1, estadísticas (Madrid, 1969), p. 17.

Total enrollments rose by 6.8 percent in the academic year 1967-1968 over the previous year. Of the major programs, the general baccalaureate showed the largest increase (20.5 percent). University enrollment rose by 10.5 percent, while students in the primary schools increased by only 3.8 percent. Most surprising was the relatively small increase in the industrial vocational training programs (2.7 percent).

The overall structure of Spain's educational system is not very different from that established and developed throughout the nineteenth century and the first decade of the twentieth century. One interesting aspect is the overlap between various levels of educational programs. Primary school is an eight-year program, but those students who are going on to secondary school, generally students from middle or upper class families, shift to a separate program (elementary baccalaureate) after four years in primary. Thus, from age ten through thirteen, some students are completing four years of primary school (generally in public schools) while others are completing four years of an elementary baccalaureate program (generally in private schools) which leads directly into the secondary school program for a superior baccalaureate. A youth who completes his eight years of primary school and then decides to study for a bachelor's degree, must take the last two years of the elementary baccalaureate, thereby losing two years of study.

The vocational training programs may be entered either after the sixth or eighth year of primary school but no time is lost in the choice. The various vocational training programs are generally five years' duration) one can enter three-year normal school or intermediate technical programs. Entrance to higher education requires one year of study beyond the baccalaureate.

Another interesting aspect of the Spanish educational system is the size of enrollments in the non-state schools. In the primary schools about 30 percent are in church or private secular schools; in the secondary schools about 75 percent are in non-state schools, and in higher education only a very small percentage. In general, the pressure to establish private educational facilities is great because of the shortage of space in the public educational system. There has always been the general obligation of the state to furnish classrooms and teachers to all students who by law were obliged to attend school. Construction, however, never seemed to keep pace with the growing demand; classrooms were crowded and quality was not high. As a result, church-supported and other private schools were established, and they generally received financial assistance from the state. While minimum standards were set by government, the quality of these private institutions varies significantly.

Because there was no obligatory school attendance beyond primary school, there were relatively few state-run facilities at the secondary school level until rather recently. Secondary education was always considered a privilege for the children of the well-to-do, and it was felt that such parents could afford to buy this education from private institutions. Thus, for example, when in 1950 the total enrollment of students for the bachelor's degree in the secondary schools was 222 thousand, only 16 percent were in state schools; and in 1966 when enrollment had climbed to about 930,000 there were 23 percent in state schools. But even when the private school facilities are considered, there are not sufficient seats in the classrooms for all the students who are prepared to pay. The government has established two categories of private schools based on quality categories. "Recognized" schools can give yearly exams, and their students only must revalidate their bachelor's degree at the end of the program by taking a state exam in an official (state) school. The second category of private schools is called "authorized" schools, and students enrolled here are called "free" students (estudiantes libres), which means they are free to attend or not to attend classes. This category was established because of the recognition that classroom space was not sufficient, and that in fact most "authorized" schools did not have classroom facilities and most "free" students did not attend classes. These students were required to take yearly exams given by state schools. In 1950, "free" students represented

22 percent of the total enrollment for the bachelor's degree; by 1966, the number had risen to 34 percent. Thus, about on-third of the student body was probably not attending classes.

In order to get a somewhat clearer picture of the educational system, details are presented for some of the important levels of the system.

Primary Education

While pre-primary schooling is not obligatory, there has been a significant growth of nursery schools and kindergartens over the past few years, especially in the private sector. The government interest in such programs is that they are preparatory for primary education and ease the transition of children into the obligatory educational system. There has also been strong social pressure for the creation of nursery schools and kindergartens as a result of the increasing number of women entering the labor force; the government has recognized that the lack of pre-school institutions is an obstacle to the working mother, and brings about problems in the care of children whose mother is forced to work.[8]

The first law of obligatory school attendance was passed in 1838, but it was not until 1857 that age limits of six to nine were fixed. These limits remained until 1900 when the upper age was raised to twelve years. It was only in 1965 that the age group of six through thirteen was required to attend school. Despite the law, however, it is estimated that at least 15 percent of this age group are not enrolled in any type of education.[9]

Pre-primary and primary school enrollment has increased gradually over the years. Despite these increases in enrollment, however, the percentage in public schools has declined substantially while the proportion in private schools rose. Starting with a proportion of 76.3 percent in 1954, the public schools declined erratically until they reached 69.3 percent in 1967. The church schools are a major part of the private school system. (See appendix table V-3.)

One possible measure of quality of education in the number of students per teacher, and in the public schools the decline has been from forty-two in 1954 to thirty-two in 1967. The private schools, on the other hand, have shown a slight rise in the size of enrollment per teacher.

Internal migration has had a serious impact on the enrollment problem. It is estimated that in any one year, about 1.5 percent of the population change residences. This movement of population has a double impact. Certain places have substantial increases in their school-age population and it becomes urgent to build new school facilities. On the other hand, some places lose school-age population, and it is necessary to shut down facilities and regroup the school population.[10] The government finds it difficult to forecast, with any degree of accuracy, the flow of these population movements with reference to locations, numbers, and ages of school children involved.

A study of the shortages of classroom space indicated that as of January 1968 there was a deficit for over 414,100 youths from age six through thirteen. This represented about 9 percent of the population in that age range. This study went on to indicate that if the shortage of school space were to be eliminated during the period of the Plan II (1968 through 1971), about 820,400 additional spaces would have to be built during that four-year period.[11] This total was broken down as follows:

Deficit on January 1, 1968		414,100
Needs due to natural growth, 1968-71		154,200
Needs due to migratory movements		252 100
	Total	820,400

In view of the fact that classroom spaces for only 50,000 youths were constructed in 1968, there was little likelihood that the deficit could be eliminated by the end of 1971. For that matter even if the government doubled its construction rate of classroom spaces to 100,000 per year, it would not be eating into the deficit that existed at the start of 1968.

The lack of space in the school system for children of compulsory school age is unconscionable. And when the shortage represents about 10 percent of the relevant population, there is little doubt of the direct loss to society and to the economy. To this, of course, must be added the question of the quality of education about which there has been considerable discussion. If the expenditure of money, time and effort in the primary education system is considered an investment in human capital formation, one may well question the economic wisdom of the investment.

Secondary Education

Secondary education in Spain encompasses a wide range of programs which in general require the completion of the obligatory eight years of primary education[12] and which are below the university level of education. There apparently are various types of classification of educational levels and programs, and various government organizations and reports use different groupings. As was shown in table 20 of this chapter, the Ministry of Education classified student enrollment data for the entire educational system by having two groupings between primary and higher education: (1) secondary (énseñanza medias), and (2) intermediate (énseñanza media superior). In the same report, a more detailed presentation of statistics for the various programs in secondary education included two of the three programs that had been classified as intermediate, but then excluded one that had been previously included as a secondary program.[13]

In a recent report on the educational system of Spain, the Ministry of Education described the structure of secondary education as including the following:[14]

1. Lower and higher baccalaureate, both general and technical
2. Pre-university course
3. Vocational training
4. Commercial education
5. Intermediate technical schools and other training programs.

The same report presents secondary education statistic by type of program that appears to differ from the structure listed above. The classification of programs is shown in table 21, and the enrollment in these programs totaled 1,154,825 in 1965 and 1,485,086 in 1967. For some reason this structure of secondary education did not include art schools and a social welfare assistant program, whose combined enrollment in 1967 was close to 46,000. No matter what the classification, students in the baccalaureate programs are by far a majority in secondary education, representing close to 80 percent of all students at this level. Because of their size and importance for higher education, a more complete analysis of the bacalaureate programs is presented here.

1. *General Baccalaureate*
The general baccalaureate program, the means of transition to the university system, consists of a four-year lower program and a two-year higher program with specialties in letters and science. Passing the final exam for the lower baccalaureate degree permits a student to enter the higher program. Passing the final exam for the higher baccalaureate degree permits a student to enter the one-year pre-university program. Upon completion of this course, an examination known as "Pruebas de Madurez" (maturity tests) is taken, and this, in effect, is the university entrance examination.

The number of students in the general baccalaureate program has increased very rapidly over the past ten years, rising from 420,852 in 1958 to 1,119,803 in 1967. While the lower and higher degree programs showed tremendous increases in enrollment, the number of students in the pre-university course rose relatively modestly, only doubling over the ten-year period. One notes sharp drops in the number of students as one moves from the lower to the pre-university course. (See appendix table V-4.)

The weeding-out process in the baccalaureate program is a rigorous one, as shown on appendix table V-5. Not only are the programs difficult, forcing students to drop out along the way, but final exams for each level have regularly failed a large proportion of the students who took the exams. For the lower level baccalaureate, the percentage of passing students ranged from a high of 55.6 percent in 1961 to a low of 44.7 percent in 1967. At the higher level baccalaureate, the success rate was slightly greater, but even here the percent passed did not hit 54 percent in either 1966 or 1967. The pass rate at the pre-university level has not gotten to 50 percent since 1959, and was as low as 40 percent in 1963.

TABLE 21

STUDENTS ENROLLED IN SECONDARY EDUCATION,
1965-66 AND 1967-68

	1965-66		1967-68	
	Number	Percent	Number	Percent
General Baccalaureate (lower and higher)	834,290	72.2	1,119,803	75.4
Technical Baccalaureate	48,288	4.1	61,946	4.2
Normal School	64,316	5.6	69,110	4.6
Commercial	20,543	1.8	24,280	1.6
Vocational Training Industrial	119,188	10.4	135,942	9.2
Technical Schools	62,101	5.4	65,380	4.4
Assistant Health Technician	6,099	0.5	8,625	0.6
TOTAL	1,154,825	100.0	1,485,086	100.0
(Art schools)[1]	(40,214)			
(Social Welfare assistants)[1]	(1,719)			

1. These programs were not included in the original classification of secondary education as presented in Ministerio de Educación, *La educación in España*, p. 61. However, these programs were included in a series of statistical tables for all programs of secondary education, in Ministerio de Educación, *Datos y cifros de la enseñanza en España, 1969*, pp. 57 and 63.

Source: Data for 1965-66, in Ministerio de Educación, *La educación en España*, p. 61; data for 1967-68, in Ministerio de Educación, *Datos y cifros de la enseñanza en España, 1969*, pp. 41-71.

With apparently such strict standards one is likely to assume that almost all those who got through the earlier hurdles should have no trouble in the pre-university course. However, even at that level the flunk rate was very high. That the examination process is an exceedingly tough one is obvious, but whether the exams serve the purpose of weeding out the unqualified is not too clear. As will be seen in chapter VI, the completion rate in the universities is not very high.

Another way of looking at attrition in the secondary school program is shown on table 22, where the calculations were made with statistics from various official sources. Here an effort is made to follow a cadre of first-year students in the lower baccalaureate program through the final exams for the higher baccalaureate degree. Thus, in the academic year 1951-1952, 58,168 students registered in the freshman class of the lower baccalaureate program (a four-year program), and at the end of the academic year 1954-1955, only 33,845 passed the exams for the lower baccalaureate degree, or 57.6 percent[15] of the original entering class. Column (c) shows the proportion of each entering class that received their degrees, and the percentages run from the mid-60s to the low 50s.

Those who received their lower baccalaureate degree were eligible to enter the higher baccalaureate program the following academic year. Thus, all 33,485 students who received their lower baccalaureate degree at the end of the academic year 1954-1955 were eligible to enter the

TABLE 22

STUDENT ATTRITION AT DIFFERENT LEVELS OF THE BACCALAUREATE PROGRAM, 1951-1967

Academic Year	New Students in first year of Lower Baccalaureate (a)	Students who passed exams for Lower Baccalaureate Degree (b)	Percent (b) of (a) with three year lag (c)	New Students in first year of Higher Baccalaureate (d)	Percent (d) of (b) with one year lag (e)	Students who passed exam for Higher Baccalaureate Degree (f)	Percent (f) of (d) with one year lag (g)
1951-52	58,168						
1952-53	62,972						
1953-54	67,920						
1954-55	75,643	33,485	57.6				
1955-56	82,597	40,546	64.4	23,802	71.1		
1956-57	99,955	39,229	57.8	24,817	61.2	18,543	77.9
1957-58	97,260	43,243	57.2	25,832	65.8	18,170	73.2
1958-59	99,708	44,258	53.6	26,848	62.1	20,519	79.4
1959-60	101,579	53,751	53.8	27,701	62.6	22,526	83.9
1960-61	111,826	59,371	61.0	32,309	60.1	23,570	85.1
1961-62	135,196	67,071	67.3	39,803	67.0	26,918	83.3
1962-63	159,653	62,058	61.1	42,103	62.8	29,217	73.4
1963-64	175,733	71,108	63.6	46,817	75.4	28,213	67.0
1964-65		76,850	56.8	50,212	70.6	31,521	67.3
1965-66		78,956	49.4	58,778	76.5	30,737	61.2
1966-67		95,549	54.4	65,593	83.1	35,702	60.7

higher program in 1955-1956, but only 23,802, or 71 percent, actually did enter. Column (e) shows the percent entering of those who were eligible, and there is a wide variation. There seems to be an upward movement during the past two years.

The 23,802 entering students to the highest level baccalaureate program in 1955-1956, Column (d), were the maximum who could receive the higher degree at the end of the following year, 1956-1957, but in fact only 18,543, or 77.9 percent, did receive the degree. See columns (f) and (g). Since about the early 1960s the percent receiving the higher baccalaureate degree has been declining, and in the academic year 1966-1967, the percent was 60.7 percent.

Tracing through these various steps in table 22 gives fairly clear evidence of the relatively high attrition among students in the baccalaureate program. If one followed the entering class of 1951-1952 directly through to those who received the higher degrees six years later at the end of 1956-1957—column (f) as a percent of column (a)—the proportion of graduates of the maximum eligible was 32 percent. In the more current years, the percentage was markedly lower. Of the 135,196 in the entering class of the lower baccalaureate program in 1961-1962, only 35,702 or 26 percent got their higher degree six years later, in 1966-1967. And if we think of the baccalaureate program as the transitional stage for the university, one should note that after obtaining the higher baccalaureate degree students must complete one additional year of schooling, the pre-university course, and the failure rate at that stage is over 50 percent.

Despite the importance of baccalaureate programs for higher education, state-run schools at this level have always served a relatively small proportion of the students enrolled. In the academic year 1958-1959, official students represented 16.6 percent of total enrollment; by 1967-1968, the proportion had increased to 26.1 percent. Notwithstanding this gain, enrollment in the state-run institutions was still a relatively small minority of the total. In 1967-1968, the number of students in church schools represented 31.5 percent (an important drop from the 40.9 percent in 1958-1959), and in other private schools, 10 percent. The so-called "free" students represented about one-third of total enrollment throughout the 10-year period.

As was indicated earlier, the "free" student registers for a program, but he has no obligation to attend classes or courses; for that matter, in many situations there are no classes for him to attend. The large number of such students is the result of a substantial gap between the demand for secondary education and the existing possibilities to meet it, especially in the official centers. This "free" education, which originally had been provisional, was later changed into a permanent status for the student, apparently because of the continuing shortages of space and facilities. However, despite the official recognition given these "free" students, there is relatively little involvement by the State in determining the qualifications of the professors who advise and direct this gradually increasing body of students. The most outstanding characteristics of "free" education are as follows: [16]

1. The program is unregulated, and the number of centers and teachers, as well as their qualifications, is unknown.

2. There is no official involvement, except for the final examination, and consequently teaching is mainly oriented to taking and passing the examinations. Although according to the law the Ministry of Education may intervene in this type of education through inspections, in practice this is difficult to carry out.

The exact number of centers of this type is not known, but it has been estimated at about 3,000. At times, there is only one teacher for all the subjects in three or four grades. Dropouts and repeaters are numerous, and many students take the exams two, three, and even four times.

The Ministry of Education recognizes the problem of the "free" student and has indicated the need to reduce the number of such students as quickly as possible through the establishment of additional centers of education.[17] The government is well aware that the introduction of the "free" student concept has given many youths, who otherwise would have been precluded from secondary education, the opportunity of obtaining the job-important baccalaureate degree. Without the concept of "free" education, youths from low-income families who were obliged to work at age twelve or fourteen, had no real possibility of continuing their education; and those in isolated or rural areas, without the necessary finances for room, board, and possibly tuition in a private secondary school, were also precluded from attendance by the system. The "free" education widened the opportunities tremendously, and there is no real likelihood that any serious attempt will be made to eliminate this educational concept. Efforts are being made to build facilities at a more rapid pace, but so far the rate of construction has not cut the proportion of "free" students significantly. Plans are being worked on for greater regulation and control of "free" education, but this is likely to be an exceedingly slow process, with little assurance of success.

Overall, "free" education has meant a significant relaxation of quality control in education, but this has been more than offset by the increased opportunities for education that the concept has offered youths who otherwise would not have obtained a secondary or a university education.

One rather oversimplified measure of quality is student-teacher ratio. In 1958, the ratio was sixteen students per teacher in official schools and fourteen in private schools, a minor difference. By 1966, however, the difference had become substantial: the ratio was thirty-one in official schools and only seventeen in private institutions. In 1951, both types of schools had the identical ratio of eleven students per teacher.[18]

Since the late 1960s there has been a growing concern about the quality of the secondary school teachers, the vast majority of whom had only the academic university program in their specialty, such as history or literature, but no courses in education. Teachers in the state schools must have a university degree, but in the non-state institutions only a a small proportion must have the university degree. The Ministry of Education has begun developing alternative plans for improving the quality of teachers, but the Ministry is also concerned with other improvements such as (1) the planning of the teaching; (2) preparation of the classes; (3) the guidance of students on methods of study; and (4) the development of diagnostic tests and control of the learning period.[19]

2. Technical Baccalaureate

Up to this point in secondary school education we have been discussing the general baccalaureate program which offers a bachelor's degree in either letters or science.[20] Another part of the secondary school program is the technical baccalaureate, which is basically nonvocational and is a general prerequisite for architecture and engineering at the university level.[21] The total numbers involved are relatively small; in 1966-1967, the size of the technical baccalaureate was only about 6 percent of the general program. Total enrollment in the technical program increased substantially over the years, rising from over 14,000 in 1959-1960, to over 55,000 in 1966-1967. In the former year, a majority of the students were studying agriculture, with only about 10 percent (all females) studying administration, which covered tourism and secretarial work. In the following years a drastic shift occurred, when the numbers in administration increased manifold and represented 32 percent of total technical enrollment. Since then, administration has risen to about 40 percent, and agriculture has leveled off at close to 33 percent. (See appendix table V-6.) What is surprising is that the proportion of students in agriculture (33 percent) is markedly higher than in industry (25 percent). The study of industry covered machines and tools, mechanics and electricity of automobiles, productivity and industrial organization, and electronics.

In 1961 about two thirds of enrollment in technical baccalaureate programs was in official centers, but by 1966 the number of students in the official schools declined to about 55 percent of total students. The number of students per teacher in the technical baccalaureate programs has been quite low, ranging from 7.4 in 1960-1961 to 10.2 in 1966-1967. The student-teacher ratio in the official schools has been considerably higher than in other schools; in 1966-1967, official schools had 25.2 students per teacher while the other schools had only 5.9 students per teacher.[22] If size of class is a measure of quality of education, it is clear that these technical programs have quality, although the official schools have been losing ground in recent times.

3. *Normal Schools*

One other part of the secondary school program is the normal school, the minimum education required of teachers in the primary schools. The baccalaureate degree is required to enter normal school and the program is three years, the last of which consists of practice teaching. A graduate of normal school is eligible to enroll at the university.

Over a ten-year period enrollments in normal schools rose by over 75 percent from about 40,000 in 1957-1958 to about 70,000 in 1967-1968. (See appendix table V-7.) Most students are registered in state schools, with about 10 to 15 percent in non-state schools. During the same ten-year period, the number of professors rose only by about 10 percent; in state schools the number of professors actually declined by about 28 percent, while in non-state schools the number more than doubled. The overall ratio of students per teacher rose from seventeen in 1957-1958 to twenty-seven in 1967-1968, a substantial rise but the ratio still does not appear excessive. However, in the state schools the ratio increased by about 150 percent, to a high of about fifty-four students per professor; in non-state schools the ratio declined from 6.2 to 4.6 students per teacher. The difference between the two types of schools is significant, and the tentative conclusion one can draw is that the quality of education in the non-state schools is better than in the state schools. There may be, of course, offsetting factors.

In 1966-1967, close to three quarters of those taking the final exams passed. Of those who completed the three-year normal school program, 4,000 were males and 8,300 were females. The pass rate in the state schools were markedly lower than in the non-state schools—about 70 percent compared to 90 percent.

It appears that the supply of primary school teachers coming from the normal schools does not meet the annual need. While the number of graduates has been rising at about a rate of 10 percent a year, many females never enter the labor market and many leave after a relatively short period of time. Also, a growing number of males and females are entering the university after completing normal school, rather than teach in the relatively low-paying primary schools.

Vocational and Technical Education

As in most industrialized and semi-industrialized countries, vocational and technical education in Spain ranges from the very formal, structured, state-run training programs for traditional skills and trades to the informal, on-the-job training programs run by private firms for their own employees. The Ministry of Education has the responsibility for many of the state-run programs, and in its recent study of Spain's educational system, the Ministry does make note of many of the problems with vocational and technical education.[23] The study recognizes that society does not rank vocational training highly, and that such training has little value as a means for social mobility. Much of the training efforts are in the industrial sector, while little has been done for training of the new skills and positions needed in the growing service sector. And even though the agricultural sector has been shrinking, there is still a need for trained agricultural workers and technicians in the modernized part of agriculture. The study comments that in the industrial sector, vocational education has been focused on traditional occupations, especially in the electrical and mechanical branches, and little attention has been paid to the new branches of industry and to new production machines and techniques. The specific needs of the labor market and of production are often overlooked, and, for example, the specialty most often repeated in vocational training schools is that of lathe operator, in spite of the surplus in this occupation at the present time. This is undoubtedly because the lathe is an old and simple tool, and therefore the most common one in the workshop.

The report of the Ministry of Education goes on to note that because of this relatively rigid training system, nonformal programs of vocational education became fairly common. For example, on-the-job training, separate from the legally established system of apprenticeship, probably produced the greatest number of skilled workers for the Spanish labor force in activities such as agriculture, construction, and office work. And private formal education also covers many gaps in the state-run system. This is particularly important for many new occupations, especially in communications. Individual private business firms as well as public organizations have also established programs of vocational training, to meet their own specialized needs.

There is relatively little information on these private efforts at vocational training, and the analysis that follows is basically of state programs and those of the church and regular private schools which meet government-established standards.[24]

Vocational and technical educations can have broad meaning, covering a wide range of educational programs. We are covering here those programs specifically referred to as vocational training and the middle-level technical schools (escuelas técnicas de grado medio) on the basis that these programs are concerned principally with preparing students for employment. Excluded from this analysis is the technical baccalaureate, which is geared principally to prepare students for subsequent schooling—either the middle-level technical schools or the high-level technical institutes (escuelas técnicas superiores),[25] which prepare professional architects and engineers.

The number of students in vocational and technical programs has expanded considerably over the years, rising from 65,000 in 1956 to almost 199,000 in 1966, an increase of 200 percent. The largest relative increases were shown in agricultural and nautical training programs, but neither of these two categories represented much more than about 1 percent of total enrollment in vocational and technical education. (See table 23.)

TABLE 23

NUMBER OF STUDENTS IN VOCATIONAL AND TECHNICAL
EDUCATION, 1956-57 TO 1966-67

| | Total | | Vocational Training | | | Middle Level |
	Number	Index 1956-57= 100	Agricultural[1]	Nautical- Fishing	Industrial	Technical Education
1956-57	65,194	100.0	452	321	44,863	19,558
1957-58	65,036	99.7	852	366	41,550	22,268
1958-59	70,088	107.5	937	345	43,908	24,898
1959-60	91,176	139.8	1,134	260	54,972	34,810
1960-61	108,908	167.0	1,275	470	63,411	43,752
1961-62	124,334	190.7	1,401	561	74,091	48,281
1962-63	137,723	211.2	1,249	504	84,570	51,400
1963-64	161,813	248.2	1,275	664	101,121	58,753
1964-65	176,955	271.4	1,754	948	108,246	66,007
1965-66	188,778	289.5	1,811	1,139	119,188	66,640
1966-67	198,601	304.6	1,835	2,231	125,577	68,958

Source: Comisaría del Plan, *Enseñanza y formación profesional*, pp. 15-16.

1. From other sources it appears that these figures represent only those students in "advanced" programs, beyond the three-year apprenticeship.

The largest group of students were in industrial training programs (over 60 percent), while the next largest (about 35 percent) were in middle-level technical schools.

The vocational training programs in agriculture are offered by official, private, and sindicato organization schools, with the latter representing about 50 percent and the official schools about 10 percent. There are two levels of training, the lower is for apprentice-journeyman and the higher is for master craftsman-foreman. In 1967, there were about 10,000 youths in the apprenticeship program and about 2,000 in the foreman program.[26] In the past few years numerous agricultural extension programs were begun, and it is estimated that about 40,000 adults attended short courses, and another 1,250,000 agricultural workers had had some contact with agricultural extension programs during 1967.[27]

While the number of young persons being trained for various specialties in agriculture seems small, it is difficult to judge the demand for technically trained personnel. Young and capable youths trained in modern technology and science can have an important impact on agricultural productivity, but how many such youths can be absorbed by a rapidly shrinking agricultural sector is debatable. The rapidly expanding programs in adult education and farm extension may be sufficient to meet Spain's needs for technically qualified persons in the agricultural sector.

The vocational training in nautical-fishing is offered principally by the state through its office of merchant marine, although private institutions also offer training programs. The programs provide training for the various deck and engine-room occupations, as well as maintenance, and cover both merchant and fishing vessels. The number of students involved in these programs is not large, but the programs have grown substantially. Enrollment has ranged from about 2,000 in 1957 to about 2,700 in 1967.[28]

It is difficult to measure the needs for such trained personnel, but the merchant and fishing fleets of Spain have been growing. In addition to various training centers run by the sindicato organization, the church, and private organizations, which enroll about 1,100 students in such training, there are four state centers that have capacity for over 2,000 students, and five state-run nautical schools with capacity for about 4,600. An additional fifth vocational training center is being built.[29] In view of this continuous growth of training capacity, one could probably conclude that the demand for trained personnel for the merchant and fishing fleets has been growing more rapidly than the supply.

Vocational training for the industrial sector is by far the largest part of the total vocational training effort of the country, and its importance is indicated by the various types of sponsors of such training centers. The state schools enrolled 32 percent of the trainees but private centers enrolled 28 percent, the church centers, 18 percent and the sindicato organization, 17 percent. The church centers and private centers have shown the largest percentage increases, and only the centers of the sindicato organization have not grown since 1960. The recent growth rate of total enrollments in all programs has been about 5 percent or less, but it is difficult to determine if this low rate is a reflection of a shrinking demand for such skills.

The industrial vocational training programs are divided into three levels. The first is a two-year pre-apprentice program which can be entered after six years of the obligatory eight years of primary school. About one quarter of total enrollments in industrial vocational education are enrolled at this pre-apprenticeship level. The apprenticeship level, which is a three-year program, enrolls two thirds of all students in industrial training. Completion of this phase gives the youth a journeyman's classification, with a certificate indicating successful completion of the apprenticeship program. For many youths this is the end of their formal education, and they then enter the labor force. Some, however, go on to a third-level program, consisting of two more years of training. This leads to the "maestría" level, or the craftsman-foreman. Less than 10 percent of total enrollments are involved in this level, but the numbers have risen significantly over the past few years. The number of graduates from the apprenticeship and craftsmen levels has risen substantially since 1963, and it would seem that the dropout rates (using rough estimates of freshman enrollments with the appropriate lag for the years of the program) were not especially high. (See appendix table V-8.)

The most popular branches of vocational training were metal (53 percent), electrical (21 percent), and drafting (10 percent). The distribution among the various branches did not differ greatly between the apprenticeship level and the craftsman level. Of the total graduates from apprenticeship in 1966-1967, 52 percent had studied metal trades, such as mechanics, metal construction crafts, and foundry work. Another 20 percent of the apprentice graduates had studied electrical installation and electric motor winding. In view of the substantial increase in automobile sales in the past few years, it seems surprising that a larger number of students are not studying to be automotive mechanics and electricians. Only 392, or 2.6 percent of all the graduating apprentices had specialized in the automotive industry.[30]

The number of students attending middle-level technical schools has increased markedly over the past ten years, as indicated in table 24. This level of technician (beyond the journeyman-craftsman) has principally been a terminal point in education for most of its graduates, but a number did go on to the higher education engineering institutes. In view of the growth of the industrial sector in both size and technical sophistication, one would expect a substantial surge in the demand for technicians and engineers. The growth in enrollment in the middle-level technical schools undoubtedly reflects this demand. However, despite the substantial size of enrollments, the number of graduates has been relatively small, implying a high dropout rate. Using rough estimates of freshman enrollments, with an appropriate lag for the three-year program, completion rates have run about 20 to 25 percent. While there is no information on what happens to the numerous dropouts from this program, one can hazard a guess that a good deal of waste of resources was involved.

The number of teachers in these middle-level technical schools has increased, but has not kept pace with either enrollments or number of graduates. As a result, the number of students per teacher rose from 13.2 in 1957-1958 to a high of 20.6 in 1966-1967. The most popular area of study is industry, which encompasses technician specialties such as mechanical, electrical, chemical, textiles, metallurgical, electrical machinery, and chemical processing and installation. Sixty percent of the enrollees and 62 percent of the graduates had specialized in this area. Architecture was the second most popular area of study (about 15 percent), and agriculture was third (9 percent). Except in these three areas, the number of graduates is too small to be significant.

Vocational Training for Adults

One of the earliest developers of vocational training programs, both for youths and for adults, was the Sindicato Organization. The basic act which set up the Sindicato Organization on June 8, 1940, granted it the authority to concern itself with vocational training and the proper distribution of manpower. Its basic duty was to prepare plans for

TABLE 24

ENROLLMENTS, GRADUATES AND TEACHERS OF MIDDLE LEVEL TECHNICAL
SCHOOLS 1957-58 TO 1966-67

	Students		Graduates		Teachers		Number of Students per Teacher
	Number	Index 1957-58= 100	Number	Index 1957-58= 100	Number	Index 1957-58= 100	
1957-58	19,714	100.0	1,951	100.0	1,495	100.0	13.2
1958-59	22,226	112.7	2,090	107.1	1,612	127.8	13.8
1959-60	31,451	159.5	2,620	134.2	1,793	119.9	17.5
1960-61	39,910	202.4	2,957	151.5	2,024	135.3	19.7
1961-62	43,996	223.1	2,945	150.9	2,291	153.2	19.2
1962-63	47,279	239.8	2,645	135.5	2,501	167.2	18.9
1963-64	55,709	282.5	4,253	217.9	2,940	196.6	18.9
1964-65	61,447	311.6	5,256	269.4	3,385	226.4	18.2
1965-66	63,382	321.5	5,292	271.2	3,116	208.4	20.3
1966-67	66,353	336.5	5,403	276.9	3,223	215.5	20.6

Source: Comisaría del Plan, *Enseñanza y formación profesional*, p. 83.

vocational training and to promote the creation of suitable institutions. In 1946 government regulations gave the Organization the responsibility for the investigation of occupational needs, the vocational training of future workers and of adults, and the establishment of vocational training centers. The Sindicato Organization has become fully involved in training, and has built many institutes and schools for the vocational training of youths and adults.[31]

In 1940 the Sindicato Organization built its first training school. The growth of vocational education, however, was rather haphazard until 1955 when the Ley de Formación Profesional (the Law of Vocational Training) was passed. The law set guidelines for programs and listed about forty specialties that were to be trained. The government completely financed vocational education, and no students in such programs were obliged to pay for any part of their training.[32]

Throughout this postwar period occasional adult training programs were offered. It was not until 1957, however, that adult training programs began to grow largely as a result of the accelerated training programs for adults started by the Sindicato Organization. This program, Formación Profesional Acelerada (FPA), was especially geared to training of very narrow skills, in short programs, for those adults who move from farm to city with absolutely no industrial skills. Other government agencies also became involved in various aspects of adult education and training.

Since 1964 there has been some general efforts at planning of adult training, but it was in 1969 that a national plan was adopted in which the Ministry of Labor acts as coordinator and financier of all vocational training of adults in Spain. All formal adult courses are free, and the

Ministry of Labor's Program of Promotion of Workers Vocations (PPO) has become the principal agent for planning training courses and programs across the nation.

The Ministry of Labor's Intensive Vocational Training Program (FIP) had been started in 1961 with the idea of using the idle facilities of public and private training schools for six-month upgrading programs. This program has largely been replaced by the PPO, which owns its equipment and facilities.

Because of the nature of the various types of adult vocational programs, and the variations in the length of the different courses, accurate statistics are very scarce. Each program seems to keep its own set of statistics, and there is no formal collection agency for the statistics. As a result, it is difficult to determine the general impact of these training programs on the labor market.

One source furnishes the following statistics for 1967:[33]

Ministry of Education	
a. Cultural courses (typing, shorthand	
and other secretarial skills	9,165
b. Vocational Education	43,000
Ministry of Labor	
a. PPO	42,108
b. FIP (including Sindicato	
Organization's Accelerated	
Vocational Training)	40,000
Correspondence Courses (only those	
related to vocational training	47,200
TOTAL	181,473

Another source shows the following statistics on the adults trained during 1968:[34]

PPO	33,000
Ministry of Agriculture	25,000
Ministry of Army	15,000
Ministry of Education	1,000
Maritime Institute	3,000
Sindicato Organization	5,150
Labor "Universities"	1,200
TOTAL	83,350

This is a far cry from the previous set of statistics. And according to an official journal of the Ministry of Labor[35] the PPO trained 72,637 in 1967 and 116,039 in 1968.

In addition to the problem of accurate statistics on the number of adults trained there is also the problem of what is being offered or considered as a vocational training course. Probably close to 100 different specialties are offered by one or another adult training program, and the variation in course duration ranges from the very short to the long. Adult vocational education covers unskilled persons who have never worked, unskilled farm hands who have never held an industrial job, unskilled industrial workers seeking some skill, technologically or otherwise unemployed workers seeking a new occupation or trade, semiskilled and skilled workers seeking an upgrading course, and many other groups.

An estimate of that part of the labor force that holds an unskilled position and has not completed any special studies is about 3.8 million persons. If one is concerned about giving each adult the maximum opportunity for human resource development, one could conclude that these 3.8 million persons need some type of vocational training.[36] Another way of estimating adult training needs is to consider the movement of agricultural labor to the industrial and the service sectors of the economy. This internal migration would require the training for the service sector of 60,300 persons to the skilled level, and 15,300 to the semiskilled.[37]

Whether the various training organizations and programs can train the estimated number of adults that need training is moot. What is clear is that there is no overall plan pinpointing the detailed manpower needs, by occupation, of the expanding industries of the nation. Specific adult training courses are given because they have been given for the past ten or twenty years, and there is little or no labor market information to indicate the kind of change needed. There is no reliable follow-up of completers of training courses to determine whether or not they find jobs in the related areas of the training. However, there is little doubt that such adult training courses have aided the transition of many workers from the declining agricultural sector to the expanding industrial and service sectors.

The Universities

This section briefly presents the basic statistics of higher education in Spain, leaving for the next chapter a complete analysis of structure, government, and quality of the university system. By so doing, we are not attributing to high-level manpower a critical position in the current economic posture of Spain. For that matter, a more likely conclusion for Spain in its current stage, or phase, of development is that shortages of various skilled craftsmen and technicians are having a greater dampening or restricting effect on the economy than is any shortage of high level manpower. However, higher education requires a long lead time. In the near future, Spain is likely to attain an economic level close to that of other Western European countries, and then the prime focus will likely be on the quantity and quality of the output of higher education. Unless the university system prepares itself now for the problems of the future, it might then be the prime bottleneck in growth potential of the country.

Higher education in Spain is composed of a university system plus technological institutes offering programs in architecture and various branches of engineering. The general rules applicable to universities are also applicable to the engineering institutes, and the differences are principally in the names of the two parts of higher education. As shown in table 85, total enrollment in higher education has risen markedly since the mid-1950s, but the very rapid rise occurred since 1961. University enrollment is about three times that of the engineering institutes, but the latter have been growing more rapidly. Since 1961 the number of students in the institutes more than doubled; over the same period, enrollment in the universities grew by about 85 percent.

TABLE 25

TOTAL ENROLLMENTS IN HIGHER
EDUCATION, 1956-57 TO 1967-68

	Total		Universities		Engineering Technological Institutes	
	Number	Index 1956-57= 100	Number	Index 1956-57= 100	Number[1]	Index 1956-57= 100
1956-57	66,659	100.0	62,215	100.0	4,744	100.0
1957-58	70,262	105.4	64,281	103.3	5,393	113.6
1958-59	71,372	107.0	62,985	101.2	4,901	103.3
1959-60	76,362	114.5	63,786	102.5	6,803	143.4
1960-61	77,123	115.6	62,105	99.8	15,018[1]	316.5
1961-62	82,331	123.5	64,010	102.8	18,321	386.1
1962-63	88,352	132.5	69,377	111.5	18,975	399.9
1963-64	102,855	154.3	80,074	128.7	22,781	480.2
1964-65	112,647	168.9	85,148	136.8	27,499	579.6
1965-66	125,879	188.8	92,983	149.4	32,896	693.4
1966-67	141,408	212.1	105,370	169.3	36,038	759.6
1967-68	154,285	231.4	115,590	185.8	38,695	815.7

1. A change in the law in 1960 resulted in a change in definition, to include students in preparatory courses and programs as registered in technical institutes of higher education.
Source: Comisaría del Plan, *Enseñanza y formación profesional*, p. 85. For 1967-68 data: INE, *Estadística de la enseñanza superior en España*, Curso 1967-68, pp. 17 and 37.

Enrollments in the university system varied significantly among the professional schools, as shown in appendix table V-9. Over the period from 1956-1957 through 1967-1968, the number of students in science rose by three times, in philosophy by four times and in economics by more than five times. Enrollments in medicine moved erratically, but did show an increase in the twelve-year period. In pharmacy, law, and veterinary science enrollments fluctuated widely, and in general showed declines, although the trend in each seems upward in the most recent years. Significant as statistics on total enrollments are figures on the number of students who complete their studies. (See appendix table V-10.) The whole university system graduated only 8,280 students in 1967-1968, about 50 percent more than the number who graduated in 1956-1957, while enrollment had risen by 85 percent during the same period. Of the total graduates in 1967-1968, about half were in the traditional professions of medicine, law, and pharmacy, while only 16 percent were in science, 10 percent in economics, and about 23 percent in philosophy and letters. In view of the size and the recent growth of the labor force, the number of university graduates entering the for-hire market of the industrial sector seems small.

Enrollments increased more rapidly in the technology institutes although there was considerable variation among the specialties offered. (See appendix table V-11.) Architecture showed the greatest increase, from 1779 in 1961-1962 to 8,158 in 1967-1968. The enrollment in telecommunication tripled over this period, while naval engineering, highway engineering, agronomy, and aeronautics doubled enrollments. Other engineering specialties showed increases of about 50 percent or less.

The number of graduates from the engineering institutes does not appear large, in view of the total market. (See appendix table V-12.) The largest single group was industry engineers, with specialties in acoustics-optics, electricity, mechanics, metallurgy, industrial organization, chemicals, technical energy, and textiles. However, the total number of such graduates in 1967-1968 was 737, a rather small number in view of the enrollment.

It would seem, in terms of the general statistics of enrollments and graduates of higher education, that the university system and the engineering institutes must not only expand its output, but also reorient priorities according to the planned or expected demands of the growing sectors of the economy. Less emphasis should be given to the traditional professions while placing greater emphasis on the more modern professions and specialties that have been evolving in recent times. These would include specialties such as electronic engineering, marketing, business management, systems analysts, and urban planners.

VI

The System of Higher Education

The Spanish university system can trace its origins back several hundred years to the founding of Spain's first university in Palencia in about 1211 a.d., and its transfer to Salamanca a few years later. The University of Salamanca became world known for its excellence, and through this, other educational institutions were founded on the Iberian Peninsula. The independence and power of the universities fluctuated over the centuries, but it was not until the late eighteenth century that a formal unified university system was established. Copying the pattern of France, the Spanish universities adopted the civil servant-bureaucratic system of organization known as the Napoleonic university. This meant that the university was organized on the model of a centralized state civil service, whose professors were government bureaucrats with professional titles to university chairs and whose organization was dependent upon a hierarchy of political power.[1] In the 1800s government intervention and interference in the universities were commonplace, and on numerous occasions they were at the point of being shut down.

Since the late eighteenth century the Spanish university system has been based on government regulation and control, as well as complete financial support by the government. Traditions within the universities either do not change, or change very slowly. Most universities are still functioning in the strict style of a Napoleonic university, with a rigid structure and organization, and a relatively limited and inflexible teaching program. Except for some minor reforms the educational system has remained the same as that of the past century. While this organization scheme may have had historical merits, it seems to be out of place in modern times with the current functions that universities now serve. On this score, two specific points can be made:[2] (1) science and its related fields are not organizable on the model of bureaucratic work, but clearly require initiative, responsibility, liberty; and (2) the Napoleonic organization makes the university a political instrument, depriving it of freedom and autonomy.

The university system has not been free of political interference and pressures in recent years. From 1939 on, the Spanish university has been pressured into a position that is not uncompatible with a rightist conception of the principles of the Falangist movement. Four kinds of measures have been employed to attain this end:[3] (1) a "purification" of the teaching staff in which the ideology of an accused professor was weighed as much as his political conduct; (2) the requirement, from all those who are to enter the permanent university faculty, of a "certificate of allegiance" to the Movement; (3) in the competition for professorships, adjusting the composition of the tribunals with persons who are "ideologically secure"; and (4) the establishment of an obligatory course called "political development," taught by professors named by the Movement. While much of this has eased up, especially since the 1950s, numerous professors have recently been sanctioned and others forced to leave the university for political reasons.[4] As recent as 1965, for example, five professors were subject to serious sanctions by the government, ostensibly for disciplinary reasons, but actually for political reasons; three were expelled from their university jobs and two were suspended for two years.[5]

There is considerable evidence that highly qualified persons who were known to be in opposition to the government did attain university professorships through open competition, but such persons generally had to be far superior than their competitors. Even if the system were subtly rigged it would be exceedingly difficult in an open competition to turn down a superior contender in order to select a mediocre person because of his politics. There is little doubt that politics plays an important role, but the system of professional appointments is such that it would be exceedingly difficult to judge whether an appointment was based principally upon ability or upon politics.

The University Structure

As is common in many countries, the baccalaureate degree is awarded at the completion of an academic program at the secondary school level. Education at the university level is geared to specific professional training, similar to the professional graduate schools of law and medicine in the United States. Except for architecture and the various branches of engineering in technological institutes (Escuelas Tecnicas Superiores), all state-recognized high-level professions are taught in "faculties" (Facultades), which are the professional schools within a university. At present there are three private universities and fifteen state universities, three of which have been established as recently as June, 1968, as so-called autonomous universities. The three private universities are relatively small, and enroll about four percent of the total enrollment at the university level.

Within the broad framework of educational policy laid down by the government, the administration of each state university is in the hands of a rector who is appointed by the Minister of Education and Science. How independent a role the rector plays varies considerably, and depends upon his own political strength and connections. Within a university each faculty is administered by a dean who is appointed by the Minister of Education at the recommendation of the rector. The rector generally recommends one of the candidates nominated by the faculty's full professors. How independent a dean is in administering his faculty will also depend upon his political support and the support he has from his full professors.

This formal structure indicates a government of the universities that has remained practically unchanged for over 100 years. Developed when the universities were dealing with very small numbers of professors and students, the structure now seems to grant inadequate authority to those handling a tremendously expanded body of professors and students. Academic authorities have sometimes found themselves with little authority except that resulting from their academic and personal prestige, and they have no effective means to back up their decisions with respect to students and faculty.[6] Under a series of government rules and regulations, various committees such as the *Claustro Universitario,* the *Junta de Gobierno,* and the *Junta de Facultad,* were created with advisory powers in the university system. The composition and authority of these committees and boards have not been clearly defined, and they have not been of assistance in the efficient administration of the universities.[7] The Ministry of Education readily admits that the job of these administrative boards has been made even more difficult by excessive centralization, and an example given is that tribunals to evaluate doctoral theses must be named by the Ministry.[8]

While the formal structure of university administration gives relatively little authority to the teaching staff, over the years the full professors have assumed more and more power. The job security and the privileges which the professor receives upon his appointment to his university chair along with the esteem bestowed upon professors by the general public, give the professors considerable authority over most academic matters in the university. This assertion of authority clearly varies among faculties and among universities.

Government regulation determines the number of universities and the specific faculties in each of the universities. In the present structure of the universities there are only seven possible faculties:

1. Science, offering specialities in biology, physics, geology, chemistry and mathematics
2. Political Science, Economics and Commerce, offering specialities in political science and economics

3. Law
4. Pharmacy
5. Philosophy and Letters, offering specialities in classical, modern, Roman and Semitic philology, history, history of America, philosophy and pedagogy
6. Medicine
7. Veterinary Science

Except for the Faculty of Political Science and Economics all the others have been in existence for many years. Political science and economics were first recognized in the late 1940s as important enough to be considered a specialty in the university with its own faculty.

By law twelve university districts were established, but this was recently increased to thirteen with the creation in 1968 of the Autonomous University of Bilbao, which is outside the original twelve districts. Within a few of the districts there are more than one branch, with some faculties in one city and others in another city. In 1968 when the Autonomous University of Bilbao was established, two other autonomous universities were created in existing districts but they were independent of the then existing universities. Thus, the Autonomous University of Madrid and the Autonomous University of Barcelona were created as competitors to existing national universities in those cities.

As shown in table 26 there is considerable variation in the educational programs offered by each university district. Only in Madrid are there all seven possible faculties, while in La Laguna and Murcia there are only three. The only faculties that are found in all university districts are Science, Law, and Philosophy and Letters. Veterinary Science and Pharmacy are offered in only four of the twelve university districts. Certain narrower specialities within faculties, such as, for example, political science, biology, and American history, are found in no more than one or two universities.

Another interesting aspect of the structure of the university system is the size of the various centers. About one of every three university students is enrolled in the University of Madrid, and in all but two faculties[9] this university has more students than any other center. Barcelona, with close to 15,000 students, had about 14 percent of total university enrollment. Most of the other centers had from about 5 to 7 percent of student enrollment.

The University Faculties

One of the most serious problems in the Spanish university is the procedure for selecting and promoting professors. Selection is made through the civil service procedure of "oposiciones" or open competition, and it is assumed that the professor is a civil servant.[10] The idea that the professor is a civil servant originated with Napoleon, and it is more rigorously maintained in Spain than in France. According to one

TABLE 26

University Enrollments by University Districts and by Faculty, 1967-68

Faculties	Total[1] Official	Total[1] Free	Barcelona Total	Granada Total	La Laguna Total	Madrid Total	Murcia Total	Oviedo Total	Salamanca Total	Santiago Total	Sevilla Total	Valencia Total	Valladolid Total	Zaragoza Total
TOTAL	92,592	22,998	14,988	9,782	1,676	36,575	2,094	3,210	6,008	6,042	6,690	7,912	7,820	7,541
Science	22,296	3,300	2,813	1,750	620	8,663	629	1,123	1,124	1,484	1,544	1,651	1,366	2,159
Political Science & Economics	12,871	5,786	2,687	967	—	11,064	—	—	—	437	—	708	2,794	—
Law	11,654	4,920	1,964	1,194	364	4,616	610	988	632	604	898	845	753	1,182
Pharmacy	4,851	694	1,180	1,329	—	2,098	—	—	—	657	—	—	—	—
Philosophy and Letters	18,648	5,862	3,299	2,007	692	6,859	855	916	1,685	1,237	1,257	2,026	749	1,285
Medicine	21,715	2,225	3,045	2,535	—	3,042	—	—	2,567	1,623	2,756	2,682	2,158	2,798
Veterinary Science	557	211	—	—	—	233	—	183	—	—	235	—	—	117

1. The total column includes enrollments in private universities amounting to 5,252, which are not included in other columns.
Source: Instituto Nacional de Estadística, *Estadística de la enseñanza superior en España*, Curso 1967-68 (Madrid 1970), pp. 19-25.

Spanish author, the problem is that the civil servants in Spain perform little work, and that in few countries is the civil servant as privileged and irresponsible as in Spain; and while this irresponsibility is bad all over, it is worse in the academic life.[11]

The Spanish method of selection and promotion of professors is significantly different from that in the United States. Each full professor (catedrático) fills a specific university chair (cátedra) in a faculty of a university. The specific chairs are created and funded by the Ministry of Education, on petition of the faculty, and they are established in a specific field of study, such as, for example, commercial law, of a specific faculty. When a vacancy occurs in a chair, or a new chair is created, an announcement of the vacancy is circulated to all catedráticos of that specialty in other universities in order to solicit applications for a transfer to fill the vacancy. In general, the movement is to the University of Madrid and to the University of Barcelona.[12] If more than one full professor files for the transfer, a special commission is created to select one of the applicants. The longevity as professor is considered, as well as the relative merits of the applicants, but politics and personal friendships also play a part.[13] Changes in posts are quite frequent, since there is no required minimum stay in one university before requesting transfer to another.

When a vacancy exists which is not filled by a transfer, the position is filled by "oposiciones" or open competition throughout the nation Any person with a doctorate and at least two years of teaching or research may enter the competition. There is no set time schedule for the announcement of such vacancies, or for the competition, and a potential candidate has no assurance that they will take place on fixed, known dates, unlike competitions for other civil service positions. In some cases applicants have had very little time to prepare, while in other cases more than a year has elapsed between the announcement of the vacancy and the announcement of the date of the oposiciones.

The Ministry of Education sets up a five-man tribunal to conduct the competition, composed of three catedráticos of the discipline involved, selected in rotation, one professor selected by the Ministry among three selected by the Council of Education, and a Chairman appointed by the Ministry. The tribunal sets the date and place of the competition, which is open to the public, and all the applicants present themselves publicly to take a series of six different "ejercicios" or exercises. The first, for example, requires each applicant to present orally, in one hour, all his qualifications for the position. Each of the other applicants is then given fifteen minutes to rebut the original presentation, and the original competitor is given ten minutes to answer each of the rebuttals. Generally, the rebuttals are efforts to weaken the original presentation, but often they take on a personal and vicious slant that results in lifetime enemies. After each exercise the tribunal votes on the applicants, and a person can be eliminated at any point of the proceedings.

Other exercises include a lecture on a topic selected by the candidate and a lecture on a topic selected randomly by the tribunal from a detailed course outline presented by the applicant. Depending on the number of competitors, the process can go on for many days, and sometimes weeks. When all the exercises have been completed, the tribunal takes an open vote, and the winner is selected by a majority vote of the five-man committee. If more than one vacancy is involved, the tribunal votes for the first place, second, etc., and the winners, in the order of their selection, pick the vacancies they prefer to fill. It is not unheard of that politics and friendships play a role in the voting and it is common knowledge that in many cases the final decision has been arranged in advance. One argument made in defense of this competitive system, often by those who succeeded in the competition, is that it has limited administrative nepotism.

The associate professor (agregado) position is also filled by an open national competition and life tenure also goes along with the appointment. It should be noted that this is a new position which has been established by law in 1965. An interesting aspect of this position is that when a cátedra is vacant and cannot be filled by transfer of catedráticos, the agregados may apply for the chair. No oposiciones are held; the agregados who meet certain minimum qualifications are rated by a tribunal on the basis of written reports and recommendations. The tribunal may recommend that the best applicant be named catedratico by order of the Ministry of Education. So far, the number of faculties that have introduced this rank is small. In view of the low salary structure in the university system, the key advantage of becoming an agregado is the possibility of being promoted to a catedrático, without going through the oposiciones.

The assistant professor (adjunto) is selected through a limited competition, and no tenure is involved. Appointments are for four-year terms, renewable for an additional four-year period, at which point it is expected that the assistant professor will have passed an open competition for a higher position.[14] The competition for assistant professorship is rather a limited one, since assistant professors work directly for a specific catedrático, and the tribunal is composed of that catedrático plus two others from that faculty. Despite the tribunal, it is the catedrático who makes the selection.

The instructors (ayudantes) are the most numerous group in the academic hierarchy. They are generally appointed on a year-to-year basis by the dean of the university, at the recommendation of the full professor in charge of the course. The specific number of instructor positions is determined and financed by the Ministry of Education, at the recommendations of the faculty involved.

The authority and power of the catedráticos as a group are very strong. There generally is only one catedrático for each major subject (such as, for example, public finance), in each university, and the other lesser professors, in effect, work for the catedrático. Throughout all the faculties of all the universities in Spain in 1967-68 there were only 1,032 full professors, or about 15 percent of all university teachers. Subject to authorization from the Ministry of Education, the catedráticos as a group within the faculty determine how many associate professors, assistant professors, and instructors there ought to be, and how these are to be assigned to the various subjects taught (which means, to the various full professors in charge of the subject). Each catedrático is free to teach his courses in any manner he sees fit, to cover whatever materials he chooses, and to send in as a substitute teacher any lesser professor who was assigned to work with him. Since the system operates on a fixed-course program with no electives, each course has a captive audience. The catedráticos therefore have a vested interest in maintaining the academic system as it is; almost any change to modernize would tend to weaken their position within the university structure.

The salary structure in the university system is relatively low, even compared with salaries paid for regular civil service jobs in the government ministries. No one in the university system receives only the basic rates, which have changed little over the years. Added to the basic rate are such items as research, incentives, and full-time agreement (plena), which has been interpreted to mean about thirty hours per week. Taxes are withheld at the source, so salaries are normally quoted as net after taxes. Including these standard extras (but not family allowances), the average net monthly salaries after taxes (in 1969) would approximate the following:

Professor[15]	33,000 pesetas	($472)
Associate Professor	25,000 "	($357)
Assistant Professor	15,000 "	($215)
Instructor	6,000 "	($ 85)

All these are paid for fourteen months a year, an extra month's pay in July and another at the end of the year.

In the vast majority of cases the teaching schedules of university professors are such that there is considerable time for outside consulting. There are no rules forbidding professors from engaging in consulting activities or from holding a second or third job, even a government job with one of the Ministries. In some faculties large numbers of professors engage in outside activities, while in others the number of professors is small. And the average amount of money earned from outside work undoubtedly varies significantly among the different faculties. Although there are no official statistics on such earnings, it was estimated[16] that in Madrid the outside income per month of economics professors averaged the following:

Professors	60,000 pesetas	($857)
Associate Professor	30 - 35,000 "	($428 - 500)
Assistant Professor	20 - 25,000 "	($285 - 357)
Instructor	10 - 15,000 "	($142 - 215)

There is concern in many educational circles about the "part-time" devotion of the university professor to teaching, basic research, and professional writing and about the low salary structure in the university. However, the prestige of the professor (especially the catedrático) is so great that he can relatively easily earn the equivalent of his university salary by outside work. There is a feeling that even if all university salaries were doubled, it would not motivate professors to give up their lucrative outside activities.

The University Programs

As indicated above, the fields of study offered at the Spanish universities are very limited, principally by the small number of different faculties that are available across the nation, the small number of specific faculties in any single university, and the small number of programs offered in any faculty. Education and training are offered solely for the basic and traditional professions, or careers.

Many of the new careers which the evolution of contemporary society requires, as well as many older careers or professions, are not available in the Spanish universities. A program of study for specialities in sociology or anthropology is not offered in any Spanish university. Business administration programs are not available, nor are programs in such areas as social welfare, public relations, and marketing. And within the faculties relatively few new courses are offered to meet the needs of the modern professional.

The Ministry of Education has recognized many of these defects. It readily admits[17] that the existing programs are designed to prepare students for one of the traditional professions, but not for careers that are required by contemporary society. Part of this problem can be attributed to the professors, who have the freedom to develop courses and programs in any way they wish. In addition, the method of teaching is in the same traditional way of lecture class and examination, where the classes are very large and the emphasis is on memorization of information. The student has little contact with his professor.

Three of the faculties—medicine, pharmacy and veterinary science— offer six-year professional programs while the other faculties offer five-year programs. There are no elective courses, and the plan of study for each semester of each year is fixed. In general, five or six specific courses of nine months' duration are taken each year, and they are usually courses in the specific specialty being studied. A faculty may not change any course within the program without obtaining prior approval of the Ministry of Education. Because of **the fixed nature of the programs,** all first-year students of a faculty, for example, take all their courses together, and they have no class contact with any other students. This would also hold true for second-year students, third-year students, etc. One result of this rigidity is that there is no transferability of credits from one program to another; if a student changes careers in midstream he must start all over.

Until about 1966 most courses were given in mass lectures by the catedrático or his substitute. The junior staff assigned to that professor normally did not have their own courses to teach, but performed whatever assignments the catedráticos gave them. For many catedráticos this was license not to lecture too often. In the 1960s university enrollment expanded rapidly, and classrooms became so overcrowded that in 1966 and 1967 not only were multiple sections of courses created, but the total regular program of some faculties was duplicated in the evening. This not only relieved pressure on classroom space, but also gave junior staff the opportunity of teaching their own sections. The catedrático, however, still was in charge of the course and could send junior staff to his own section at will.

Most courses are full-year courses, and frequently there are no quizzes, no midterm exams, and no term papers. The final exam is the sole criterion for passing or failing the course. In many cases the professor has his own course materials published as the text for the course, and his lectures are little more than a repeat of the textbook. It is not uncommon for only a small percent of the students of a course to attend the lectures regularly.

A student who fails one or two courses (or who fails to take the exam) in a year's program may still go on to take the next year's program.[18] This means he takes all the courses of the second-year program while making up the failed courses. Make-up exams are given a few times during each year, and there is no limit on the number of times a person may take and fail make-up exams. As a result, course failures do not seem to be of great concern to the students. If, however, a student fails three or more courses in any one year or does not take the exams, he cannot go on to the following year's program until he clears all but two of his failures. He can, however, go on if he registers as a "free" student.

Another interesting problem of higher education in Spain is the insertion of the one-year pre-university course between secondary school and the university. The establishment of this course in 1953 was motivated principally by the conviction that the preparation acquired in secondary school was insufficient. The repeated and frequent reforms of the pre-university course in 1957, 1959, and 1963 are proof of the dissatisfaction with its results. In the opinion of many professors even those students who do pass the pre-university course examination have not achieved a high enough level to continue with higher education.

Problems of Growth

The growth in higher education over the past number of years has been impressive, with enrollments doubling in twelve years, from 57,000 in 1956 to 110,000 in 1968. (See table 27.) The increases have not occurred evenly among the universities. Valencia showed the largest relative rise in enrollment (165 percent) while Barcelona and Valladolid also showed larger than average rises with 115 percent. Oviedo showed the smallest increase with a rise in its student body of only 3.8 percent.

As a result of this increased demand for higher education the government undertook a huge building program to provide the necessary facilities. While this program has undoubtedly made inroads on the space problems, there is still a substantial shortage in various faculties in the universities. No direct data on shortage of space are available, but the number of "free" students gives some indication of students who are not taking up seats at the universities. While the average of "free" students for all universities was 20 percent, the rate varied from 12 percent in Sevilla to 36 percent in Oviedo. Not all of these students, however, were "free" students because of shortages of seats in the universities.

Under the rules laid down by the Ministry of Education many years ago, "free" students could matriculate in a faculty, not attend any classes, and take the final exams. If they passed the exam, they passed the course, and they could in this manner earn their university degrees. This concept undoubtedly was started so as to permit those young persons who had to work or who had to live far from a university to attain a university degree. From the 1930s through the 1950s approximately 45 percent of the student body were registered as "free" students,[19] but the proportion has been declining since then. The overall decline for universities has been substantial, falling to 20 percent in 1967-68, although the percentage of "free" students in the technological institutes rose from 7 percent in 1960-61 to 22 percent in 1967-68. (See appendix table VI-1.)

The largest proportion of "free" students occurs in the Faculty of Political and Economic Science still about 36 percent in 1967-68. According to the Ministry of Education[20] the high rate in economics is probably due to the fact that this specialty can be studied in only six of the twelve university districts, and that it is studied to a great extent by people who are working at the same time. Veterinary science is studied by a considerable number of rural students who usually do not have the financial means to move to the three cities where the subject is offered. And with respect to philosophy and letters, it is the logical specialization by which primary school teachers can continue their jobs while obtaining the necessary degree to teach at a secondary or higher level. Also, the high numbers of failures in the system force many students to register as a "free" student in order to continue in the university program.

It is somewhat disquieting to realize that about 12 percent of the medical students and 10 percent of the science students were "free" students. (Medicine had been as high as 26 percent in 1960-61.) Since there is no penalty for failing a course other than the requirement to take the final exam again at some future date, "free" students take the chance of passing the exam and the course. The university system acquiesces in this academic game, and offers final exams a few times during the academic year. It should be noted that "free" students in the faculties of science, pharmacy, and veterinary science must show successful completion of the required "practical" work of the program before being permitted to take the final examinations.

TABLE 27

UNIVERSITY ENROLLMENTS BY UNIVERSITY
DISTRICTS, 1955-56 AND 1967-68

University Districts	1955-56 Enrollments		1967-68[1] Enrollments		Percent Increase, 1967-68 over 1955-1956	"Free" Students as Percent of Total Enrollments, 1967-68
	Number	Percent	Number	Percent		
TOTAL	57,030	100.0	110,338	100.0	93.5	20.4
Barcelona	6,945	12.2	14,988	13.6	115.8	22.3
Granada	4,998	8.8	9,782	8.9	95.7	20.8
La Laguna	920	1.6	1,676	1.5	82.2	30.5
Madrid	19,074	33.4	36,575	33.1	91.8	20.0
Murcia	1,344	2.4	2,094	1.9	55.8	28.7
Oviedo	3,092	5.4	3,210	2.9	3.8	35.8
Salamanca	3,573	6.3	6,008	5.4	68.2	16.2
Santiago	3,146	5.5	6,042	5.5	92.0	18.5
Sevilla	3,664	6.4	6,690	6.1	82.6	12.6
Valencia	2,981	5.2	7,912	7.2	165.4	17.5
Valladolid	3,638	6.4	7,820	7.1	115.0	23.8
Zaragoza	3,655	6.4	7,541	6.8	106.3	18.0

1. Includes only state run universities.
Source: Comisaría del Plan, *Enseñanza y formación profesional* (Madrid 1967), p. 93.
Instituto Nacional de Estadística, *Estadística de la enseñanza superior en España*, Curso 1967-68, pp. 19-25.

Providing additional facilities to accommodate the "free" students will not eliminate such students. There are numerous reasons for "free" students, and they will never completely disappear voluntarily. With the rise in incomes and the growth of the middle class, a large proportion of families can afford to and do send their children to the university. Thus total enrollments have risen substantially, and the proportion of "free" students has declined. However, one should not interpret this to mean that the higher educational system has become egalitarian. Despite this tremendous enrollment increase, one analyst believes that probably no more than 2 percent of university students are workers, or sons of workers, while in England the proportion is in excess of 20 percent.[21] Another analyst indicates that while the lower class represents between 62 and 68 percent of the total population, sons of unskilled workers represent under 3 percent of the total university enrollment.[22] In 1968 scholarships for university study numbered about 3,900 or less than 3.5 percent of total university enrollment.[23]

It should be noted that tuition costs are negligible, and few persons are prevented from attending the university because of the direct costs of schooling. Fees and costs of books can be somewhat of a problem, but more important are indirect costs such as the costs of feeding, clothing, and housing a youth for five years, during which time the student forgoes the opportunity of earning some income. These costs could prevent many lower income families from sending their children to the university. An earlier impediment to the low-income family sending its children to the university is the limited state facilities at the college preparatory secondary school level. About 45 percent of these secondary school children attend church or secular private schools, and the costs at these non-state schools do impose a limitation on lower income families.

The growth pattern of university enrollments varied significantly among the university districts, but the variation among the different faculties was even greater. (See table 28.) While total enrollments rose by 100 percent from 1955-56 to 1967-68, the number of students in Economics increased by over 700 percent, and in Philosophy and Letters by over 350 percent. At the same time Veterinary Science showed a 67 percent decrease, and Pharmacy and Law also showed decreases. The skyrocketing enrollments in some of the faculties undoubtedly have caused serious adjustment problems in a number of universities.

Another growth indicator is the proportion of women registered in the universities. In 1955-56 females represented 17.6 percent of all university students; by 1967-68 they represented 30 percent. In all but one

TABLE 28

UNIVERSITY ENROLLMENTS, BY FACULTY,
1955-56 AND 1967-68

FACULTY	1955-56 Enrollments		1967-68[1] Enrollments		Percent Increase, 1967-68 over 1955-56	Percent of Women Students in	
	Number	Percent	Number	Percent		1955-56	1967-68
TOTAL	57,030	100.0	115,590	100.0	102.7	17.6	30.0
Science	7,193	12.6	25,596	22.1	255.8	19.6	27.9
Political Science & Economics	2,291	4.0	18,657	16.1	714.4	6.1	20.4
Law	17,385	30.5	16,574	14.3	- 4.7	4.8	15.0
Pharmacy	6,621	11.6	5,545	4.8	-16.3	49.2	60.1
Philosophy & Letters	5,347	9.4	24,510	21.2	358.4	67.0	57.0
Medicine	15,863	27.8	23,940	20.7	50.9	5.2	16.2
Veterinary Science	2,330	4.1	768	0.7	-67.0	0.7	8.2

1. Includes both state and private universities.
Source: Comisaría del Plan, Enseñanza y formación professional, p. 91.
   Instituto Nacional de Estadística, Estadística de la enseñaza superior en España, Curso 1967-68, p. 18.

faculty the proportion of females increased over the twelve-year period; in four faculties the proportion more than tripled. It was only in the Faculty of Philosophy and Letters that the percentage fell, from 67 percent to 57 percent. Females were a majority in only one other faculty, Pharmacy, where the proportion rose from 49 percent to 60 percent.

Student Unrest

As in most countries around the world, university students were in the vanguard of Spanish political activities of the left and of the right. By virtue of their family and educational backgrounds they were the elite, or the children of the elite. The State authorities placed limits upon their activities, but in general they were not treated as harshly as one would expect in an authoritarian state. While the government could not countenance open violation of its regulations, it hesitated to crush the student activists. Various controlling actions were taken by the government to contain the student opposition to the Franco regime, but the actions were not sufficient to eliminate student activities.

Just as the government had established official sindicatos in all the sectors of economic activity in the nation, it also had established a single official organization for university students. From 1939, when the Spanish Civil War ended, until 1965 there existed a single organization for university students, Sindicato Español Universitario. In recent years it hardly represented the student body of the universities and it was generally known that many students had established informal political organizations, ranging from the far right to the far left. When these groups began open protests for political and academic purposes, the government substituted a new student organization for the old one. By decree of April 5, 1965, Asociaciones Profesionales de Estudiantes was established, but the major part of the student body continued to shun this government-established organization.

Clandestine student organizations continued to exist and to protest on various matters. Over the past few years numerous student strikes occurred, frequently shutting down individual faculties and even universities. While the issues ranged widely, a frequent issue was participation by the student body in the decision-making process of academic matters in the university.

A series of student strikes at various faculties of the University of Madrid took place during 1967-68 as well as the early months of the academic year 1968-69. Police were called in, violence occurred, and the administration closed the University for the remainder of the academic year. The problem of who passed what courses was solved relatively easily—official notices were published announcing that course exams would be held at various times during the late summer and early fall. This delayed the opening of school for about a month beyond the normal date of early October. But not all faculties opened that soon.

Many of the strike leaders were students in the Economics Faculty and much of the militancy seemed to flow from this faculty. When the Ministry of Education announced the delayed opening of the University, it noted that because of overcrowded conditions, construction of new buildings had been started in the summer of 1968 for the Faculty of Political Science and Economics, but had not yet been completed. The political science section was to be temporarily housed in a building located across a principal highway which would separate these students from the other faculties. The economics section was to be located in new buildings in Somosaguas, a surburban area about six miles beyond all the other faculties of the University of Madrid. Telephone facilities between this Somosaguas campus and Madrid were very limited, and it was almost impossible for a student to make a phone call. This, of course, precluded these students from being leaders in any student movement. Public transportation to and from the main campus was provided, but the 30-minute bus ride and the wait between buses made the Somosaguas location quite distasteful for most students. These new facilities were not completed when the other faculties opened for the academic year, and it was not until early December 1969 that the Economics Faculty held its first classes of the academic year.

While the official reason for the construction of the new buildings for the Economics Faculty at Somosaguas was overcrowded conditions, many persons saw other reasons: to punish the students (and perhaps also the professors) of this faculty for the past events, and to make it exceedingly difficult for these students to be leaders of future demonstrations and strikes. It was true that many of the faculties were overcrowded, but it was generally felt that the new facilities for Economics could have been built adjacent to the existing buildings on the regular university campus in Madrid. Also, plans had already been made for the establishment of a new university in Madrid, the Autonomous University, which was scheduled to have an Economics Faculty. This undoubtedly could have relieved some of the pressures of the increasing student enrollments.

With the opening of the academic year 1969-70, police were stationed at the entrance of each building and at various points on the campus (both Madrid and Somosaguas). Students had to show matriculation cards to gain entrance to any university building. All political meetings on the campus were broken up by the police, and it was suspected that police in civilian dress attended classes to spy on the activist students. These police activities were irritating to the students, and a key demand in many of the student strikes was withdrawal of the police from the campus. The students were also concerned about the quality of their education and the right to participate in the decision-making process of the university. Varying degrees of student unrest existed in different faculties, and because of strikes, students in some faculties missed as much as half of the scheduled class meetings.

Student unrest has undoubtedly affected the university administration, as well as the quality of the education. In the short run, it would appear that the quality had deteriorated. However, if the numerous strikes have some impact on courses and the organization of faculties, there could easily be a marked improvement in the quality of education in the long run.

Quality of Education

Speaking on "The Crisis of the University," don José Botella Llusia, the rector of the University of Madrid, pointed out many of the faults of the university system and how they contribute to the low quality of university education.[24] He noted that the professors devote more and more of their time to outside work, and that low university salaries contribute to the situation of "pluriempleo," or dual job holding. And in reference to the selection of professors by the system of open competition, the rector observed that too often the judging tribunal has decided on the winner before the competition begins. Referring to the student body, he commented that the quality of the students coming to the university was low, and this, combined with the exceedingly large numbers, made quality education in the university difficult.

In a sample survey of the opinion of university graduates living in Madrid[25] a majority were not satisfied with the number of professors, nor with the professor's dedication, scientific competency, and teaching abilities. Nor were they satisfied with the relations between teacher and students. And only about 10 percent of those interviewed believed that the university develops good professionals or scientists; basically, what the university provides is the "title" which permits a person to practice his profession. The university graduates rejected the system of selecting professors by open competition and they were opposed to the life-tenured university chairs; the majority interviewed felt that professors should be hired on a contract basis.

Even among the professors[26] there is general dissatisfaction with university education and a recognition of the great need for change. Classes are too large, students rarely talk to or visit with professors, little effort is devoted to research or writing, teaching salaries are too low for the professors to devote themselves to teaching. While many professors recognize the need for change, there is some doubt whether a large proportion of the catedráticos would be willing to forego many of their privileges that quality education would require.

The Ministry of Education points to the low practical content of courses as one of the most typical defects of the university.[27] Most classes are limited to transmitting theoretical knowledge, and little attention is given to real cases, clinical history, laboratory experiments, or the discussion of the serious problems of the contemporary scene. Society needs the university to develop creative minds able to respond to the challenge of new times. Social evaluation is moving very rapidly, and the university's inability to respond to new and evergrowing social needs is increasingly obvious, and creates a climate of general unrest.

While quality of education clearly extends beyond numbers of students and numbers of faculty members, the ratio of these quantities can give one aspect of the educational process. An examination of table 29 shows that there has been a decline in the number of students per professor. In the university system the figure was thirteen students per professor in 1968-69; and in the technological institutes it was 9.1 students per professor.[28] A distribution of these ratios by university faculties shows that the variation among faculties is considerable. The Faculty of Veterinary Science showed 3.7 students per professor, while the Faculty of Economics showed 34.2 students per professor. The ratios in the other faculties ranged from about thirteen to twenty students per teacher, figures that do not seem particularly high in an absolute sense. In the technological institutes the ratios were even lower than in the university faculties. The range for the various specialties was from a low 4.5 students per professor to a high of 14.0 per professor, clearly ratios that would appear to be acceptable for quality education.

Despite these low student-teacher ratios there is considerable criticism of the quality of university education. The numbers may make possible quality education, but they do not automatically result in quality.

Dropout rates may also be a clue to the quality of education, although reasons for dropouts may vary from finances to personal and family problems. However, the variation in rates among the faculties and the branches of technological institutes indicates that factors within the educational system are significant. (See table 30.) In the universities the dropout rates ranged from 20 percent to 40 percent, and in the technological institutes from 23 percent to 64 percent. Quality may be a factor, but the difficulties of the program or the grading systems are likely causes for such wide ranges in dropouts. In most units of higher education the dropout rates of official students were markedly lower than those of "free" students. Since "free" students are frequently full-time workers with only limited time for study, higher dropouts are not to be unexpected.

Survival rates in various programs of higher education also may give some clue to the quality of education, although here again such rates may be affected by numerous other factors. Table 31 shows survival rates for various programs, computed with an appropriate time lag to take account of the normal years of each program. The variation in survival rates ranged from 14 percent for economics to 95 percent for agronomy, and only four programs had rates of under 50 percent. There seems to be no basis on which to conclude that a low (or a high) survival rate indicates a high quality program.

In view of the absence of objective criteria which measure quality of education, there is little basis to compare the quality of universities and

TABLE 29

NUMBER OF STUDENTS AND PROFESSORS
AT UNIVERSITIES AND TECHNOLOGICAL INSTITUTES, 1960-61 THROUGH
1968-69

| | Universities | | | Technological Institutes | | |
	Number of Students	Number of Professors	Number of Students per Professor	Number of Students	Number of Professors	Number of Students per Professor
1960-61	62,105	2,791	22.3	7,239	1,095	6.6
1961-62	63,810	2,968	21.5	9,472	1,306	7.3
1962-63	69,375	2,900	23.9	10,685	1,795	6.0
1963-64	80,074	3,078	26.0	11,445	2,048	5.6
1964-65	85,148	2,297	25.8	13,029	2,499	5.2
1965-66	92,983	5,174	18.0	29,353	2,375	12.4
1966-67	105,370	6,272	16.8	36,038	3,353	10.7
1967-68	115,590	7,068	16.4	38,695	3,536	10.9
1968-69	129,306	9,960	13.0	40,933	4,488	9.1

Source: INE, *Estadística de la enseñanza superior en España*, pp. 17 and 37; and Ministerio de Educación y Ciencia, *Datos y cifras de la enseñanza en España, 1970*, Tomo 1, pp. 100-103.

TABLE 30

DROPOUT RATES FOR SELECTED FACULTIES AND BRANCHES OF
HIGHER EDUCATION, FOR OFFICIAL AND "FREE" STUDENTS, 1967-68
(in percent)

	Total	Official Students	"Free" Students
Economics	40.0	38.1	48.0
Law	26.5	23.8	35.9
Pharmacy	26.5	26.1	31.1
Medicine	23.5	23.3	27.3
Veterinary Science	20.5	17.0	27.6
Architecture	44.8	43.0	53.6
Aeronautics	45.9	45.9	46.2
Agronomy	41.8	38.6	53.3
Highways	53.6	51.8	65.6
Industry	49.0	48.2	51.5
Mines	37.4	36.1	44.7
Mountains	22.9	21.9	29.0
Naval	50.1	52.0	40.4
Telecommunication	64.6	65.1	59.4

Source: INE, *Estadística de la enseñanza superior en España*, pp. 32-34, and 41-42.

TABLE 31

SURVIVAL RATES IN VARIOUS CAREERS OF HIGHER
EDUCATION, FOR 1965-66, 1966-67, AND 1967-68

(graduates as percent of students who registered
"n" years earlier, when "n" is years of the program)

	Value of "n" years	Years in which Graduated		
		1965-66 (percent)	1966-67 (percent)	1967-68 (percent)
Medicine	6	—	51	53
Veterinary Science	5	65	44	75
Pharmacy	5	64	63	77
Science	4	65	47	—
Law	5	37	36	36
Philosophy	5	39	34	62
Economics	5	15	22	14
Architecture	5	78	62	75
Aeronautics	5	68	143[1]	69
Agronomy	5	91	83	95
Highways	5	117[1]	96	39
Industry	5	70	63	46
Mines	5	48	92	75
Mountains	5	119[1]	43	60
Naval	5	72	73	88
Telecommunication	5	64	59	60

1. Rates in excess of 100 percent are possible when there are disproportionate concentrations of repeaters or of students changing their plans of study.
Source: José Luis Romero y Amando de Miguel, *El capital humano*, Table 40, pp. 238-239.

technological institutes. Since both are governed by the same administrative rules and regulations there is no reason to conclude that the quality of one is higher than that of the other.

The Autonomous Universities

That basic and drastic changes were needed in the university system of Spain has been recognized by many people for a long time. Minor changes have been introduced over the years, but they had little impact upon the system. The Ministry of Education was conscious of this need in 1962, when it organized a joint conference with UNESCO on education and the economic and social development of Spain.[29] However, it was apparent that the vested interests within the university, especially those of the catedráticos, would oppose any major or significant change in the existing university system. To avoid a direct confrontation, the Ministry of Education developed the idea of establishing the autonomous university, which would operate outside the rules, regulations, and limitations of the existing universities.

In view of the overcrowded conditions of the existing universities the Ministry of Education was in an excellent position to establish new universities. The autonomous university was to be established without the rigidities and vested interests of the older universities, and they were to have administrative authority to develop modern and flexible organizational structures and academic programs. These new institutions, if successful, would be used as models for change in the older universities.

The Ministry of Education established autonomous universities in Madrid, Barcelona, and Bilbao, and they began functioning in the academic year 1968-69. Each had a limited number of faculties, and the number and kind varied among the universities. Each of these new universities was given special authority to employ teaching staff through a university contract (as distinct from "oposiciones" and being on the Government payroll as a civil servant). Although the salary structure was identical to that of the other universities, these new universities had the flexibility of hiring at higher ranks and the authority to promote those with ability. The catedrático title, however, continued to be limited to those who acquired the title through open competition. Each faculty was authorized to limit the size of the enrollment, and to develop its own academic program. No uniform path of development was established.

The Faculty of Economic Science and Commerce of the Autonomous University of Madrid was given the responsibility of developing not only a new program in economics, but also the first academic program in business administration offered by any university in Spain. While a few non-state institutes, principally church sponsored, offered business administration programs, no university offered more than some isolated courses in this area. In its first year, this faculty at the Autonomous University of Madrid enrolled 300 students, and an additional 200 in the second year; approximately three-quarters of these students were in business administration.

This Faculty of Economic Science saw two basic aspects to its development: (1) create a modern, flexible administrative structure and program; and (2) create flexible academic programs which give students a choice of specialities that are directly related to the needs of modern society.

With reference to administrative structures and programs, this faculty created two branches, economics and business administration, each offering separate programs with specialities in each. Each major area of specialization is coordinated by a chairman, and all faculty members from full professors to assistant professors teach and have the responsibility of developing their own courses. An academic committee of faculty members and elected representatives of the students was established to determine academic matters. Student representatives also participate in the selection of students for admission and for scholarships.

Tentative academic programs have been developed in both economics and business administration. In the economics branch, there is no specializing at the undergraduate level; all students are offered a wide selection of economics courses, such as labor economics, agricultural economics, regional and urban economics, which are currently not offered in any other Spanish university. At the graduate level a wide range of specialities are to be offered.

In the business administration branch a number of specialities will be offered at the undergraduate level, including general business, financial management, marketing, and accounting. At the graduate level a uniform program is planned for all students.

This example of the Economics Faculty of the Autonomous University of Madrid indicates a possible alternative to the traditional administration and programs found in other universities. If this approach succeeds in educating and training students in the more modern areas of study and the more modern professions, this is likely to be a guide for the older universities. The Spanish economy has developed rather rapidly in the past few years and there is a substantial need for high-level manpower trained in the most modern professions with knowledge of the most sophisticated techniques and materials. The Spanish universities, however, are basically still teaching traditional courses with traditional materials to students who are being prepared for traditional professions. A significant change is necessary and the autonomous universities may be leading the way through their experimentation.

A growing number of Spanish professors have had some graduate school training abroad, where they were exposed to modern and sophisticated materials and courses. Many are prepared to teach such materials and courses if the educational system is changed sufficiently to permit such innovations. Of equal concern, however, are the specific occupational and professional needs of the nation in high-level manpower. There are no labor market surveys in Spain that indicate the supply of and demand for specific high-level manpower occupations. There are no accurate statistics on which professions are growing rapidly, and which have stopped growing or are actually shrinking; and there are practically no data on many of the newer professions and newer specialities of traditional professions. Such information on high level manpower is a prerequisite to educational planning. Change from a traditional university education system to a modern one that is responsive to the needs of society requires considerable knowledge of the trends in the labor market as well as of modern education.

Changes in the Educational System

The creation of the autonomous universities was the start of some basic changes in the education system. Some new programs were started and some of the rigidities of fixed and required courses were loosened. The administrators of the autonomous universities were given greater latitude in administering programs and in employing and utilizing professors. Whether these changes will have the impact needed to motivate changes in the older universities is yet to be seen. There already is some concern that when the catedráticos gain a bit more power in the autonomous universities they will take a less flexible position (like that of the catedráticos in the older universities) in order to protect the rights and privileges (and the opportunities for outside employment and income) that come with their position.

In its 1969 report on education in Spain, the Ministry of Education proposed various changes in the whole educational system, one of which affected the method of selection and appointment of university professors. Rather than have the government civil service system of open competition, with the winner getting a government appointment on a life-tenured position, the report proposed that universities have the right to contract directly with professors, with salaries based upon various factors that indicate experience and ability. The catedráticos are likely to try to prevent such a change or to slow down the introduction of such change.

In August, 1970, a General Law of Education and of Financing Education Reform was passed, which schedules a series of changes over the next few years. Obligatory schooling has been increased by two years, from age fourteen to age sixteen. Primary school is renamed general basic education with an eight-year program of two stages: a five-year stage and a three-year one. In the latter period some specialization is to begin. At completion of general basic education (approximately age fourteen) a student has the choice of a three-year baccalaureate program, or a vocational training program of three levels (up through technician which would require eight years beyond general basic education). There continues to be a one-year course, after the baccalaureate, before entering the university. This is now called "Curso de Orientación Universitaria," course of university orientation, which is to be developed and supervised by the university, and offered in state baccalaureate schools and in some authorized non-state schools.

Education in the university faculties and in the technological institutes is to be offered in three cycles. The first, of three years' duration is to be devoted to the study of the basic disciplines; the second cycle, of two years, is for specialization; and the third cycle, of two years, is for higher specialization and preparation for research and teaching.

Whether these changes in the structure of the educational system and the various other changes prescribed by the 1970 law will have a significant impact upon the needed supply of manpower is yet to be seen. No plans have been made to survey the specific manpower needs of the economy nor to estimate the future needs. The education at the university level is likely to improve, gradually, but many of the drastic changes that are needed are not likely to be introduced rapidly. Unplanned growth of various branches of higher education is likely to continue, although the quality of the education will undoubtedly improve somewhat.

There are many persons, in and out of the government and in and out of the educational system, who are not very optimistic about the possibilities of significant improvements in the educational system. Implementing the changes called for in the 1970 law will take many years.

VII

The Processes
of Manpower Allocation

In economic theory resources are allocated by the smooth functioning
of the market mechanism and no barriers or rigidities hinder the auto-
matic mechanism from manipulating the supply and demand in order
to clear the market. In the real world, however, there is a whole range
of factors that affect the functioning of the market, and this is especially so of labor markets. Human resources are not only affected
by various institutional factors, but also by political, social, and personal factors.

Rigidities in a labor market are commonplace, and it would be sheer
chance if the numerous labor markets in a country were cleared at any
point in time. There are, though, degrees of flexibility in labor markets, and a significant factor is whether the basic needs of employers
are met while unemployment is kept at some acceptable minimum.
However, there are no objective criteria that determine the basic labor
needs of employers, nor the acceptable minimum unemployment. In-
formed judgments based upon the particular set of circumstances are
probably the most effective way of evaluating a nation's processes of
manpower allocation.

Rigidities in the Market

The supply side of the labor market in Spain contains a whole series
of rigidities related to the educational system. As in many nations
around the world, the educational system reflects the social structure,
and for a variety of factors the different levels of education are not open
equally to all economic and social groups. The hidden "cost" of fore-
going a job and income is generally enough to prevent children of low-
income families from obtaining a university education. In Spain there
seemed to be a close correspondence between social classes and levels

of education. Primary education was seen for the lower classes, secondary education for the middle class, and university education was reserved for the upper classes. While this simplistic view of the educational system may have actually been true many years ago, the situation has changed to some degree and is continuing to change. Children of working class families do get through secondary school, and some even make it through the university. And a growing number of students from middle-class families are making it through the universities.

Whereas there was almost sufficient facilities and space for children in the state-run primary schools, this was not so at the secondary school level. For close to a majority of students attending secondary schools, it was necessary to matriculate in private schools because of the shortage of state-run facilities. And in many instances the private schools were far superior to the public schools, thereby offering wealthier children the opportunity for higher quality education. The number of university scholarships offered by the government was exceedingly small, but more than a token gesture, and while tuition was minimal, other costs plus foregone income were sufficient to exclude almost all students from the lower income groups.

The establishment of a category of "free" student did give students at the secondary and university levels a chance to go for their degrees without attending classes. This opportunity did permit some low-income students who otherwise could not have obtained an education to get their degrees. The numbers from working class families, however, were relatively small.

Cultural and social factors have had their impact on certain professions which now have high prestige. Because of the traditional outlook of esteem to professions such as doctors, lawyers, engineers, and pharmacists, large numbers of young people study these professions, regardless of demand. The average earnings of such traditional professions are not especially high, but the social prestige is, and for upper-class families the prestige apparently is more significant than the potential income. In 1969, for example, a lawyer could have earned as little as 5,000 pesetas a month ($70), and an engineer about 15,000 pesetas, while a skilled machinist could have earned between 15,000 and 20,000 pesetas a month.[2] Despite these differentials there seems to be no shortage of lawyers or engineers, but there is a relative shortage of skilled workers.

While no reliable surveys have been made to determine shortage occupations, there is a consensus on the existence of a shortage of professors and teachers, especially in the science areas, and of skilled craftsmen and technicians. These shortages have persisted for a number of years. As far back as 1962 a report on the economic development of Spain[3] indicated that the supply of trained specialists at the secondary level needed to be expanded, probably in all categories. This report noted that Spain should undertake a study to determine the numbers needed, the kinds of specialization required, the types of training establishments that would be most useful and where they should be located. This suggestion was not fully followed, and detailed information on needs is still not available.

As recently as 1968 there still appears to be a shortage of certain types of skilled workers and trained technicians, partly explained by "defective training of technical personnel and skilled manpower at all levels."[4] While there has been a growth of training facilities, the expansion has been haphazard, with various public organizations as well as private ones expanding training programs without centralized direction. Because of the high costs involved, and the possible wastage that can result, it is essential that planning be directed with efficiency and precision, and that permanent cooperation be established between the Planning Commission, the Ministry of Education, and the Ministry of Labor.[5]

In addition to the barriers of entrance to the various levels of the educational system, there also are entrance barriers to certain professions and jobs. Historically and traditionally employment with the government as a civil servant has been considered as the only employment with security. To obtain a professional job with the government meant competing with other applicants in an open competitive exam. The vast majority of university graduates sought positions with the government, and it was not uncommon for these university graduates to spend years in specialized study, in an effort to "win" a government job in these competitive exams. While a growing number are now going into the private sector, there still are many who spend years studying for competitive exams in an effort to get a government job.

Jobs in the educational system also have obstacles to easy entrance. To be eligible to teach in the primary schools a person must have successfully completed normal school, which is a three-year program after an elementary baccalaureate degree. About 15 percent of normal school students attend nonofficial schools, and they must take a special exam at the completion of their program in order to "validate" their studies. The completers of the program in the normal school receive the title "maestro," and this permits them to teach in nonofficial primary schools. To teach in the official primary schools it is necessary to succeed in an open competitive exam, similar to that given for other civil servants. Indicative of the mismatch of supply and demand for primary school teachers is the fact that in 1962 a total of 19,272 maestros took the competitive exam for 7,000 jobs.[6]

To teach in the secondary schools a person must first have a university degree. In the nonofficial schools there is no other requirement, but in the official schools an applicant must also succeed in an open competitive exam. Except for the full professor, teaching at the university level requires only a university degree. To attain a full professor position, a person must have his doctorate and must win at an open competitive exam. It is generally acknowledged that the competitive exams are often horrendous affairs which can and do keep highly qualified persons out of the system.

The rigidities of the educational system have inhibited changes that were needed to accommodate the changing needs of the society. New industries, modern managerial and administrative techniques, and technological changes are some of the factors that would require new educational programs to educate and train the employees needed by modern industry. At the university level few new programs or courses have been added over the past twenty years, and little effort is made to meet the needs of the expanding sectors of the economy. This is also true at the vocational high school level. The same vocational programs are being offered that were offered over twenty years ago, and in many schools the equipment is at least twenty years old. In general, new equipment is found only in new schools, but in some of the programs even the new equipment has become obsolete. The wood-carving program still manages to attract sufficient students. Because of the investment in equipment schools find it financially difficult to modernize their programs, and because of the absence of labor market information there is no great push to change the courses already being offered. As a result, industry has little alternative but to employ those with relatively little relevant training, and to offer supplementary on-the-job training where it is needed.

While there is no hard evidence on this point, a number of observers of the Spanish scene have drawn the conclusion that the use of relatively modern machinery and technology has been limited because of the inability of firms to locate skilled or technically qualified personnel. Obsolete machinery and techniques are sometimes used because they are what the available supply of workers can handle. If the practice of using less sophisticated technology because of a real or imagined shortage of qualified manpower is widespread, this might explain the slow reaction to train workers to handle more modern technology. Relatively low physical productivity in many Spanish industries may be explained by the skill factor of manpower, but the relatively low wages of workers do provide the industries with acceptable rates of profit. Thus, industry may have little incentive to introduce modern technology if the higher costs of employing qualified labor might offset the possible gains from higher productivity.

If increased industrial productivity has a high priority for economic development of Spain, specific manpower policies to further this aim must be developed and adopted. One option is to expand the training programs for the sophisticated skills needed by modern technology in industries that are scheduled to grow significantly under the nation's economic plans. With such skilled manpower readily available, expanding industries are more likely to introduce the modern machinery that could increase their productivity and their rate of profit. An alternative policy is to allow wage rates in certain industries to rise to a point where firms find it more economical to substitute machinery for labor. The introduction of new machinery is likely to increase the demand for highly skilled workers and technicians, and training programs (both public and private) will be developed to increase the supply.

As is true in many smaller firms in the United States, the Spanish firm is likely to have an informal source of needed workers. Connections are always quoted as being exceedingly important in getting a good job, and these connections could be family, geographic or political. Except for the very large firms, where hiring may be done in an impersonal procedure, most companies use their employees as the principal source for new workers. This type of "inbreeding" is an inexpensive method of recruiting, and also assures management that the new employees will receive the needed on-the-job training from the worker who recommended the new ones. While such an informal mechanism may work well for individual firms, it may deprive competent workers without the right connections of jobs for which they are qualified. Such unemployed persons end up in less satisfactory jobs or jobs that do not use their higher skills. If this is widespread, a significant waste of human resources is involved.

Another waste of human resources is the general underutilization of Spanish workers who return to Spain after a number of years of industrial work experience abroad. Many of these Spanish emigrants had little or no industrial experience before leaving Spain, and while relatively few of the returnees attained the skilled-worker level, many had acquired experience on semiskilled industrial jobs in technologically abvanced companies. The return for many of these workers was a disappointment. Jobs equivalent in skill level or sophistication to those held in other countries were not readily found in Spain. And even when such jobs were discovered, the returning Spaniards often would not have the right connections to get the job. Many times where the returning emigrants had accumulated some savings while abroad, he would leave the labor market and use his capital to open a small store or shop. This involves a wastage of his industrial experience, although in the short run this increase in small shopkeepers does increase the likelihood of political stability. In the long run this increase of small shops builds economic inefficiencies into the economy which after taking root are exceedingly difficult to eliminate.

"Pluriempleo," or moonlighting, is another factor which seems to distort the functioning of the labor market. The practice of holding more than one job exists in all large cities but is rather common in Madrid. Because of the relative shortage of skilled maintenance workers, such as electricians, carpenters, plumbers, and masons, many craftsmen and other workers have numerous opportunities to do extra work after their regular working hours. The opportunities are even greater for a wide range of professional workers, whose principal vocation is government employee, teacher, or employee in banks and insurance companies. Consulting with the government or with private firms is a common practice of many university professors. There is no doubt that all of this "pluriempleo" does distort the operation of the labor market. If the workers refused to engage in moonlighting, not only would the wage structure of the market change significantly but the number of persons training for such occupations would increase dramatically. Or put differently, if the wage structure changed significantly, many persons who currently engage in moonlighting would no longer do so, and this would have a positive effect upon the potential labor supply.

It is difficult to assess the impact on the labor supply of a decline in the amount of moolighting. The part-time jobs held by the moonlighters are highly skilled or professional, and very few of the unemployed are qualified to perform such work. If many moonlighters disengaged themselves from their part-time work, the wage rates for such would rise, reemphasizing the already known situation that a shortage of such skilled and professional workers exists. It should be noted, however, that many of the moonlight jobs are casual work, or on contract work, and the employers are not seeking and would not employ full-time regular employees.

Matching Supply and Demand

Full employment of human resources on jobs freely chosen is not only important for the economic and social well-being of the individual workers, but is also an important goal of the economy in its drive for a high rate of development. But absolute equilibrium between human resources and the needs for manpower is rarely attainable. To this, a report of a subcommittee on employment of the Committee on Labor of the Planning Commission stated:[7]

> One cannot imagine a perfect match, simultaneously and permanently, of the supply of and demand for work, in every province, in every economic activity, and in every level of training. Nevertheless, it has to tend continuously to this situation so that the rhythm of development of man and society is as rapid as possible.

It is at the disaggregated levels of the province, in industry, and the occupation that we have difficulty describing and analyzing the supply and the demand for labor. In general we manage to make estimates of the global picture, i.e., of the total demand for manpower and the total supply of manpower, and we then indicate whether there is shortage or a surplus. And even these estimates are based upon approximations. Statistics are available, by major industry, on the total labor force, the employed, and the unemployed. We then assume that the labor force is the labor supply, the employed is the labor demand, and the unemployed is the surplus of supply over demand.

When such figures are aggregated in this fashion (even when available by major industry branch) we are washing out differences among occupations and among geographic areas. From reliable sources we know that not all occupations are equally in excess supply, and that not all provinces have the same labor market situation. Nevertheless, because of the limitations of the statistics we act as if there were a single labor market (or perhaps a few) rather than the thousands that actually exist.

While Spain reports statistics on employment by occupation cross-classified by industry,[8] such information is only a partial description of the demand for labor. We have no information on the geographic distribution of the demand, nor do we have information on vacant positions which would represent unfilled demand. On the supply side we have labor force data by industry and occupation and unemployment data only by industry, but no distribution by geographic region. At a maximum these sets of statistics represent the current stock of the labor supply and of the available jobs. They give no indication of the growth and the changes in either the supply or the demand.

The current stock of the labor supply is more or less fixed, with only marginal changes taking place; it is constantly being diminished by deaths and retirements, and augmented by new participants. With very little information available on the occupations being vacated by deaths and retirements and on those for which demand is increasing, the potential entrants to the labor force make their choice of trade or profession haphazardly, based principally on personal preference or chance. At the vocational level many youths are trained for trades based upon openings in vocational programs, despite the irrelevancy of the trade to the labor market at that time. The vocational high schools have little information on the needs of the labor market, and they continue to offer the same traditional trade courses that have been given for many years. The students are offered no occupational counseling, and only by sheer chance are some of the manpower needs of industry met by these training programs.

At the higher education level students also select their programs of study with little information about the manpower needs of the economy and the society. Career choices are frequently based upon personal or family preference because of prestige or social esteem. Undoubtedly many university students do have some information on the potential income of various professions, and this may assist them in their career choice. However, because of various market rigidities, including social and cultural factors, potential earnings of a profession do not always reflect the employment opportunities of that profession.

A case in point is the engineering profession. Engineering has been a high prestige profession for many years, and the estimated average earnings are relatively high within the wage structure of the private sector of the economy. In the first quarter of 1969 hourly earnings of engineers ranged from a low of 55 pesetas ($0.78) in shoe manufacturing to 134 pesetas ($1.91) in cork manufacturing and in electric power, water and gas.[9] An unweighted average of all industries was 102 pesetas ($1.46), or about 21,000 pesetas per month (the equivalent of $300 at the official exchange rate). In addition, opportunities for supplementing income through moonlighting were considered to be rather good. In mid-1969 a study was published which questioned the need for more engineers and projected a surplus of 7,300 by the end of 1971.[10] This study, referred to in Spain as "Informe Matut," received considerable publicity. Using data of the Planning Commission to project the demand for engineers, the report calculated a need for 2,970 engineers over the four-year period 1967 to 1971, of whom 2,468 were for expansion and 502 were for replacement. Over this same period it was estimated that the system of higher education would graduate 10,271 engineers, for a surplus of 7,301 as of the end of 1971. Projecting requirements to 1976, the report noted that for both expansion and replacements the need for engineers between 1971 and 1976 will be about 4,400, still not sufficient to absorb all of the estimated 1971 surplus of 7,301. The report concludes that even if no engineers were graduated during the five years 1971-1976, there still would be a surplus of over 2,000 engineers on December 31, 1976.[11] In press interviews the author of the report, José Luis Matut Archanco, noted that engineers were unemployed and underemployed in 1969, and that his projected surplus of 7,300 in 1971 meant that they would be either unemployed or involved in work other than engineering.[12]

Some persons[13] questioned the statistical reliability of the Informe Matut, but the focus of the criticism was on the magnitudes involved, not the fact that a surplus was projected. Nevertheless, there was general agreement that the report would have little or no impact on enrollments in the engineering institutes. The educational system was such that those students in the pre-engineering programs of the secondary schools would matriculate in the engineering institutes if they passed the required entrance examinations. Even if such secondary school students had second thoughts about engineering careers, they were basically locked into the path leading to engineering. A shift in career goals generally meant starting the secondary school program over again.

In view of the tremendous increases in university enrollments during the past few years, it is possible that other professions may also be facing significant surpluses in the near future. Because of lead time needed to turn out a university graduate, the supply of high-level manpower can be projected with some degree of accuracy. Forecasts of manpower requirements are much more tenuous. Economic conditions may change rather suddenly, causing a shift in the demand for labor in general, or for persons in certain occupations. New technology may result in a change in the occupational mix of an industry, and the previous needs of certain occupations may be changed sharply. Productivity changes also may have an impact on the requirements of high level manpower. In addition, a relative change in wage rates may have an impact on the utilization of manpower, making long-range forecasts rather unreliable.

While all of these factors may have their impact on the economy, they do not always work in the same direction, on the same industry. The impact of one factor may offset that of another, and not all firms of an industry are affected to the same degree. In general, employment structures and employment patterns of an industry are rarely changed markedly in a short time period. Year-to-year changes in an industry are more likely to be marginal, and for this reason it is possible to make reasonably reliable estimates of changes.

Individual firms, however, are not, and need not be, involved in making industry forecasts of demands for specific manpower. A firm employs a certain mix of workers with the skills that can perform certain operations. The combination of workers hired reflect the relative wage rates of occupations that can perform the work, as well as the availability of the workers in the labor market. In most situations there is not a unique relation such that only a specific combination of workers can perform a needed operation; where shortages exist less-qualified workers are employed to perform the same tasks. There is little evidence that output in any industry has been curtailed because of the shortage of persons in a specific occupation. In view of the relative inflexibility of the educational system, tied in with the social prestige factor for some professions, it has been suggested that many Spanish firms tailor-make their technology and their operations to the available and projected supply of manpower.

Much greater flexibility was shown in the accelerated training programs for adults which were run by the Sindicato Organization. The short-term programs were begun in 1957, and were geared to the narrow skills that could be used by industrial firms in semiskilled jobs. These were especially useful for those adults who were moving from the farm to the city, with absolutely no industrial skills.

Efforts were made to establish some semblance of a formal labor market by means of a national employment service (Servicio National de Encuadramiento y. Colocación). It was thought that data collected through employment service offices would provide the basis for estimating the supply of and demand for various types of labor, by industry and by geographic areas. However, as in most countries where economies operate with some freedom, the national employment service handles considerably less than a majority of job placements. In Spain the placement rate of the national employment service was at a surprisingly low rate of 1 percent, whereas in Belgium it was 12 percent, in the United States 16 percent, in Sweden 25 percent, in the United Kingdom 25 percent, and in Germany 30 percent.[14] The tradition in Spain of having the right connections undoubtedly has contributed to the common situation where job applicants deal directly with a firm, and both employee and employer see no need or advantage to operate through the national employment service.

Efforts at Manpower Planning

In a free market economy with considerable freedom of choice there is always some wastage of resources. It is not unusual to have overproduction or underproduction of commodities, with the resulting wastage. With reference to manpower, the training of too many persons for one occupation and not enough of another may involve a waste of human resources which could have an impact upon the commodity market. Many countries feel they cannot afford a large amount of such waste, and they attempt to develop economic plans which spell out in varying degrees of detail the matching of supply and demand. Economic plans can never eliminate all excesses, but they frequently manage to keep wastage within acceptable limits.

The indicative economic planning in Spain has given the free market considerable latitude. Broad goals are established and by means of government incentives and financial policies efforts are made to attain the economic goals. While manpower and human resources are recognized by the Planning Commission as having some importance to the economy,[15] relatively little manpower planning was done in both the first and second economic plans. Nevertheless, some government agencies have been involved in various aspects of manpower which could readily lead to full-scale manpower planning.

One of the first attempts at a full-scale analysis of the manpower situation in Spain was made in 1964 by a division of the Ministry of Labor, Dirección General de Empleo. This study examined the forecasts made in the first economic plan (1964-1967) and attempted to analyze the available employment data in light of the forecasts.[18] Various gaps in statistical data were noted, but a serious effort was made to analyze the labor market and to make manpower projections. In the following year a second study was published by the same unit of the Ministry of Labor, using 1965 data and a slightly more sophisticated analysis. These two reports are still considered as the best analytic studies of manpower in Spain, although they were clearly focused on specific years. It is difficult to determine why these studies, which appeared to be the start of a series, were discontinued after two years. Two events which occurred about this time may account, at least partly, for the discontinuance. In 1964 the national statistical agency of the government, Instituto Nacional de Estadistica (INE), began a regular survey of the labor force by means of personal interviews of a sample of households throughout the nation. The data from this survey were highly reliable and provided the basis for a continuous series of statistics on the labor force. At the same time a reorganization took place within the Ministry of Labor and the Direccion General de Empleo was reorganized out of existence. There may have been no connection between two events, but by 1965 it was clear that the Instituto Nacional de Estadistica had the field of manpower statistics to itself.

Pursuant to Law 141/1963, the INE began its first survey of the Spanish labor force in 1964, based on a sample survey of interviews with 75,000 families throughout the country. It used the standard definitions developed by the International Labor Organization for the basic manpower terminology, and it used as a survey guide the survey conducted in 1960 by the six countries of the EEC. Data collected covered the general characteristics of the household, as well as the following information for each member of the household fourteen years of age and over:

1. Sex
2. Age
3. Civil status
4. Cultural level
5. Principal occupation
6. Situation within the occupation
7. Branch of industry
8. Number of hours worked per week
9. Where relevant, reasons for working less than 45 hours per week
10. Secondary occupation
11. Seeking employment: form, duration, and circumstances
12. Nature of employment being sought
13. For those who have lost or left a prior activity, a description of that activity

The original plan was to collect these series of statistics every quarter, and to publish them in a single annual report. In 1964 the report published tables for the second, third, and fourth quarters; in 1965 data were presented for all four quarters; in 1968 data on only the second and fourth quarters were published; and in 1969 only first and second quarter data were furnished.

Despite the erratic-periodicity of the data and the erratic publication dates of these reports, the statistics of the series are a major contribution to understanding Spain's manpower picture. Not only does this series present a trend of the characteristics of the employed and the unemployed, but also of the occupational structure of the labor force, cross-classified by industry. The series presents the basic manpower data which is currently used by many government agencies and by the planning commission. If any manpower planning were to be done in Spain, the statistics of the INE household surveys would be the basic data to be used.

Although the Ministry of Labor does have broad responsibilities over problems of employment and manpower training, it has done relatively little in the planning of manpower and employment. There is no specific unit within the ministry that has the responsibility of developing a methodology for manpower planning or of developing a specific manpower plan. Whether this is really a lack of interest by the top officials of the Ministry of Labor, or whether this is a reaction to the lack of interest in manpower by the Planning Commission does not matter. While the Planning Commission is controlled largely by the Opus Dei, the principal group in the government, at the present time, the Ministry of Labor has traditionally been controlled by the Falangists, the group recently replaced by the Opus Dei as the power within the government. The Planning Commission has shown no interest in manpower planning and has made no move to get the Ministry of Labor to participate in the planning effort.

There are, however, a number of persons working in different divisions of the Ministry of Labor who are interested in manpower planning and who have had some experience in manpower planning in less developed countries for the ILO or other international organizations. They have made efforts to interest their superiors in the Ministry in planning, but they have not been too successful. Various reports on the planning of employment and on methodology were drafted by staff personnel in the Ministry,[17] but there has been no success in getting the agency to act on these documents, or to use these reports as leverage with the Planning Commission to get more involved in the planning process. There appears to be little likelihood in the near future that the Ministry of Labor will be asked by the Planning Commission to participate in the planning process.

In an indirect manner the Ministry of Education did become involved in the problems of manpower and manpower planning, from the supply side of labor. In 1969 the Ministry issued a study of education in Spain,[18] commonly referred to as "Libro Blanco" or the White Book, which the Ministry considered as providing the bases for an education policy. In analyzing the education structure the report did note its important function of developing human resources, and proposed some major changes in the education system in order to raise the quality of education, improve its flexibility, and open the higher levels of the system to the lower income groups. In the report the Ministry of Education did make an attempt to plan for the supply of manpower, but it failed to consider the demand side of the market. As is often the case, the educators became so involved in the process of education, i.e., in improving the quality and the quantity, that they failed to take into account the market demand for the specialized manpower that is produced by the educational system. Thus, the White Book makes projections of high level manpower, in terms of the graduates of the university system and the technical institutes, without planning for new programs and new professions that are needed in the industrial marketplaces.

The Ministry of Education's White Book was not intended as a effort at manpower planning, but it must be considered defective when it develops a program for education without serious consideration for the demands of the labor market. Little concern was shown about the need of the system to introduce new professions, new intermediate technologists, and administrative specialists.[19] And little was done to mesh the proposed changes in the educational system with the economic plans of the Planning Commission. Despite such criticisms, however, the White Book has provided a basis for improvements in the educational system.

The Ministry of Labor's involvement in vocational training has grown substantially in the past number of years. Its Programa de Promocion Profesional Obrera (PPO), which is to promote vocational training for adults, is the basic coordinating organization for training outside the regular educational system. Tens of thousands of adults go through short-term training courses which prepare them for some unskilled or semi-skilled industrial work. The kinds of courses offered were not based upon any analysis of market demand, but upon custom, tradition, and a "feeling" by some administrators of what types of work were available. In 1968, however, a group of researchers were set up in PPO to engage in the planning of training programs. In November 1969 this group did present to the director of the program a completed report,[20] in which forecasts were made of the 1970-1971 needs of vocational training of adults for positions in agriculture, industry, and services. In general, the methodology used to make these forecasts was to take the employment trends for occupations cross-classified by industry, extend them into the future and then adjust for replacement needs resulting from estimated quits, retirements, and mortality rates. These short-run forecasts are likely to be reliable because sharp shifts in employment trends do not occur very frequently. These forecasts, therefore, may be of value for adult retraining, where the training time is short, but not for the training of youths where a number of years are involved.

Because of the limited purpose of this PPO study, it made no attempt to relate its forecasts to the Economic Plan. However, it did develop a methodology that might prove of value to longer run manpower planning. Further planning in the PPO, however, it not likely to occur. One, the research was a one-time thing and the research team was disbanded after the report was completed. And second, the impact of the research on the actual operations of the PPO was slight, because of the relatively high costs of changing training programs.

In developing its economic plans, the Planning Commission did create a series of industry boards and specialized panels on subjects such as education, productivity, and labor, all of which were to submit reports to help the Planning Commission formulate the plan. While most of these board reports were published by the Commission, the one by the Labor Panel was not,[21] apparently due to dissatisfaction and disagreement by some members of the panel with parts of the draft report. The Planning Commission undoubtedly did see the draft report, but nevertheless it did not see sufficient merit in the basic concepts of manpower planning to incoporate such planning in its global economic plans. It accepted the ideas that the educational system should improve and expand, and that employment will undoubtedly grow. But the economic plans produced by the Planning Commission made no effort to project the manpower needs of the expanding industries not to project the potential supply to be produced by the educational and training systems of the nation.

The Labor Panel had established a subcommittee on employment which submitted a draft report to its creating agency on the prospective manpower situation. This subcommittee report did analyze the labor market and did make projections on needs and potential resources, by broad occupational groups, for the four years 1967-1971 of the second Plan. (See table 32.) It is difficult to evaluate the projections, but the statistics do present a basis for developing an educational and training program to approach the estimated manpower needs of industry.

TABLE 32

AVERAGE ANNUAL MANPOWER NEEDS AND POTENTIAL
RESOURCES OF THE EDUCATIONAL SYSTEM, 1967—1971
(in thousands)

Occupational Groups	Manpower Needs	Potential Resources of the Educational System
Managers	0.0	—
High-level technicians	9.1	8.9
Middle-level technicians	17.3	16.6
High-level white-collar employees	8.1	6.5
Middle-level white-collar employees	32.2	52.1
Low-level white-collar employees	47.9	85.3
Master craftsmen and foremen	44.9	4.4
Skilled industrial workers	149.5	242.9
Semiskilled workers	—1.9	95.9
Unskilled workers	-145.5	—

Source: Report of Subponencia de Empleo (1967), unnumbered pages, and reproduced in unpublished report of Ponencia de Trabajo del II Plan, 1968-71, p. 16.

An examination of the projections made by the subcommittee indicates relatively slight shortages for high-level technicians, middle-level technicians, and high-level white-collar employees. Large annual shortages are foreseen for master craftsmen and foremen. For semi-skilled and skilled industrial workers and for low- and middle-level white-collar employees the report forecasts that the potential resources produced by the educational system will exceed the needs of industry.

In general, these projections are in line with the various estimates of relative manpower shortages made by knowledgeable persons in the labor field. The degree of accuracy of these projections is not as important as the concept of manpower projections, which are basic to manpower planning. There are various techniques for projecting manpower requirements and manpower supply, and each has its strong and weak points. And the merits of one technique over another may vary with the conditions in the nation doing the planning.

In view of the pace of Spain's economic growth during the 1960s it seems unlikely that the country can continue its rapid economic growth without hitting a manpower bottleneck in the near future. The labor markets in Spain are not very flexible, and its educational and training systems are too rigid to produce readily the trained manpower needed by the modern industrial sectors of Spain's burgeoning economy. Only by manpower planning will it be possible to orient the educational system to an interest in helping to serve the manpower needs of the nation's economy.

VIII

Summary and Conclusions

The focus of this study has been on the institutions and factors that have affected the development of human resources in Spain, and on the role manpower has played in the economic changes of the country. While the viewpoint appears narrow, it still permits a broad perspective of the growth and development of modern Spain. Manpower is only one factor of many that affects and is affected by changes in the economic, political, and social structure of a nation.

While Spain is still a dictatorship, under the rule of Francisco Franco, significant political and economic changes have taken place over the past thirty years. Franco still retains overall control but the day-to-day governance has gradually been shifted from the traditional groups that supported Franco during the Civil War (the military, the Falangists, and the conservative Christian Democrats). In recent years the control of Spain's government has been chiefly in the hands of Opus Dei, a lay Catholic organization, which established the nation's goals of economic growth and development within the framework of a competitive, capitalistic economy. The shift from a nationalistic, self-sufficient society started with an opening to foreign investment and to tourism. Then, with economic planning, the nation pushed for rapid industrialization and for Spain's acceptance in the European common market.

These significant shifts in economic policy did result in a rapidly rising level of national income, placing Spain within the range generally considered semideveloped. Numerous modern industries were developed and expanded, and mass production of a wide variety of modern consumer products made available for a rather large percentage of the family units such products as automobiles, televisions, hi-fi sets, and washing machines.

Such economic gains did allow considerable economic mobility, but relatively little change occurred in the social and political spheres of the nation. The rigidities in the social structure remained, and little effort was made by the government to force social change. There was an increase in the degree of political freedom, but it was rather slight, and it appeared to be given merely as a token in order to gain greater acceptability by other western European nations. There is never any doubt that Spain is ruled by an authoritarian government, with final power in the hands of Francisco Franco.

Summary of the Development of Manpower in Spain

Within the milieu of an authoritarian government sponsoring rapid industrialization through foreign investment and a capitalist, market-type economy, the demand for manpower shifted from agriculture to industry. Economic policies for both the public and private sectors fostered a decline in the agricultural sector and a growth in the industrial sector. The resulting migration to the urban centers caused the usual shortage of facilities in the cities with a concomitant rise in prices. But the manpower problems in neither the agricultural sector nor the industrial sector were solved.

1. The efforts to cut back resources in agriculture were based on the assumption that productivity in this sector was very low. Policies which, in effect, forced persons out of agriculture employment did not, however, increase farm productivity significantly. Those remaining in the agricultural trades continued to use the traditional technology, and until recently little effort was made to modernize this sector. Only in the last few years have attempts been made to improve the technology and to use more scientific methods of production. This shift in policy means a change in the demand for agricultural labor. The growing need is for labor trained in the modern technology and modern scientific methods of agricultural production.

2. From the mid-1950s onward Spain's economic policies and plans fostered industrial growth and development. The manpower needs of these new firms and industries varied significantly from the traditional labor generally employed previously. In addition to the usual semi-skilled industrial worker who is quickly and easily trained for his repetitive job, there was a burgeoning demand for a host of skills that previously had hardly existed in Spain. With the development of a variety of industries manufacturing consumer durables, there was a growth in the demand for technicians and skilled craftsmen to design and build the products, along with the demand for skilled maintenance workers and repairmen. The growing use by industry of new methods and technologies meant an increased demand for a variety of scientists and engineers.

3. In addition to the growth of the industrial sector there was growth in the service sector that also resulted in an increased demand for specialized manpower. Enrollments in the school system, from primary school through the university, expanded sharply during the 1960s, increasing the demand for teachers at all levels of education. Banks, insurance companies, as well as wholesale and retail trade grew rapidly with a concomitant rise in demand for manpower. During this period of growth, tourism expanded from a minor industry to one of the major service industries, and accounted for a significant share of the growth of foreign exchange. As a labor intensive industry, tourism's growth meant a substantial rise in the demand for manpower in a wide range of semiskilled and skilled service occupations.

4. The regular sources of the supply of labor were in no way geared up to satisfy the specific manpower needs of the new and rapidly growing firms and industries. Where industry's manpower requirements were for the traditional skills, the expanding educational and training system did manage, with a lag, to meet the needs. However, while the government policies and plans called for an expansion of educational and training facilities and teachers, there was practically no detailed planning for the match of industry's manpower needs and the normal output of the educational system. Expansion of education meant increasing the output of the system without examining or questioning the composition of the output. The vocational training schools continued to turn out graduates with the same traditional skills that had been produced during the previous thirty years. The technical institutes and the universities also continued to educate students for the same traditional professional and technical occupations that existed in the educational system for decades. The supply of trained and educated manpower did increase, but not necessarily in the right amount for specific occupations, or in the right occupational mix.

5. The formal structure of the educational system and the bureaucracy that developed within the system have made any significant change exceedingly difficult. Rigidities and obstacles exist in many parts of the system, and the vested interests of the faculty inhibit modernization of programs. The shortage of public educational facilities at all levels, but especially at the secondary (college preparatory) level, has forced the more affluent families to send their children to private schools which often provide higher quality education than the public system. And in some situations there literally is insufficient space in the public schools, forcing children of low-income families to do without primary education or college preparatory education. While this limitation at the secondary school level seemed to have been used in

the past to limit college preparatory education (and therefore university education) to the upper-income families that could afford to send their children to private schools, efforts are currently being made to change this policy. The building of facilities has increased significantly, as has the program of teacher training, but the demand for education seems to be rising at the same pace.

6. The quality of the education in the public system and in the universities is generally recognized as poor to fair. Quality at the primary and secondary levels is frequently bought in private schools by the well-to-do, but there are very few alternatives to the state-run universities. It is possible that some increase in quality will result from the government's current policy to increase facilities and increase the numbers of scholarships to children from low-income families. At the university level some efforts are being made by the government to weaken the bureaucratic power of the faculty by creating new autonomous universities with greater flexibility in employing professors and in developing educational programs. It is too soon to evaluate the overall impact of these new autonomous universities, but some changes do appear to be improvements.

7. Despite all these efforts by the Ministry of Education to change and improve the educational system, there has been little attention focused on the manpower needs of the marketplace. In a very limited area, that of the need for teachers at different levels and in different specialties, the Ministry of Education has programed expansion to meet the teacher needs of its own system. However, at the university level there has been no planning to restructure or redesign the traditional programs so as to meet the manpower needs of new professions or of old professions with new cores of knowledge. For that matter, neither at the Ministry of Education nor at the Planning Commission has a serious effort been made to determine the skills and occupations needed by the marketplace, where the public and private sectors, as well as the stagnant and expanding industries, compete for the limited supply of skilled and trained manpower.

8. Formal vocational training was always considered as the basic education for the children of low-income families, and the costs of this training were underwritten by the state, whether in public or private schools. Vocational training programs are offered by the Ministry of Education, in the public schools, as well as by church organizations, the Sindicato Organization, the Ministry of Labor, and private, for-profit organizations. None of the students in vocational training programs have tuition costs; some students also receive scholarships covering living costs, tools, uniforms, etc.

9. In general there appear to be sufficient vocational training facilities to meet the demand, but here the problem is in the vocational programs being offered. Young men are generally being trained for the same traditional occupations as were their fathers, with the tools and techniques of decades back. Past investment by schools in machinery and equipment has been high, and replacement with modern equipment is generally too expensive. More tragic, however, is the fact that no labor market surveys have been conducted to learn the manpower needs of industry. Vocational training schools are regularly graduating numerous lathe operators, despite the fact that they are a glut on the market. Youths trained in wood working or in wood carving find little need for their skills in the expanding industries of the nation. Firms in the more modern industries frequently find it necessary to train their own manpower, despite the years of "training" many job applicants have had.

10. Because of the migration from the agricultural to the industrial sector, and because of efforts at modernizing the agricultural sector, a tremendous need arose recently to train and retrain adult workers. The rural workers who migrate to the city need training in industrial skills, while the rural workers who remain on the farms need retraining to handle the technology of modern and scientific farming. In recent years the Ministry of Labor has developed a large-scale program to offer short-term courses for such training and retraining of adults. In many instances mobile training facilities are utilized, and they are brought to the village or town where the training is to be given. The Ministry of Labor has engaged in some short-run manpower projections, based upon the economic plans of the Planning Commission, in order to help determine the type of training courses to be offered to adults. These short-term adult training courses have been relatively successful in giving workers a skill needed in the labor market. And while tens of thousands of adults have gone through such programs it has been estimated that there are many more thousands who should be exposed to such training.

11. While the economic planning of Spain is similar to the indicative planning of France, the planning in Spain is much more directed in the public than in the private sector. Planning in the semipublic tourist industry was quite important, since this industry was the most successful in bringing foreign exchange into the country. With considerable assistance and participation by the government, tourist facilities expanded rapidly, and the need for trained manpower quickly became obvious. The government established training programs specifically for the manpower of this industry, from maids, waiters, and cooks to language experts in order to man the tourist offices in every significant-sized city in the nation. These training programs

were geared directly to the needs of the tourist industry, and they were quite successful in matching the labor supply with the industry's demand for trained manpower. It should be noted that this was a rather unique case, and the government was nowhere as successful in any other industry.

12. In general, while economic activity expanded at a healthy rate, the supply of trained manpower did not match the specific needs of industry. Untrained manpower and persons trained for unwanted skills became part of the unemployed labor force. And many agricultural workers who migrated to the industrial centers found that they lacked the industrial skills to compete for the available jobs. This mismatching of supply and demand for specific skills is shown not only by unemployment, but also by a significant amount of moonlighting. It was estimated that in Spain about 19 percent of white-collar employees and 12 percent of blue-collar workers hold more than one job, while in Madrid the percentages are significantly higher.

13. The official unemployment rates are low, at about 2 percent of the labor force. Because of the relatively heavy demand for labor in many western European nations during the 1950s and 1960s, substantial numbers of Spanish workers, many unemployed, left for work abroad. It is generally conceded that Spain's low unemployment figures are partly due to emigration to Western European countries, which helped stabilize Spain's labor market. The data indicate that the net emigration of Spanish workers over the past ten years totals more than 4 percent of the labor force. If these emigrants had remained in Spain, the unemployment rate is likely to have exceeded 6 percent. In view of the operations of Spain's labor markets over the past ten years either these emigrants, or an equivalent number of other workers, would have been unemployed.

14. In the broadest terms, Spain's economic plans did refer to manpower, such as noting that the expansion of industry X will mean an increase of employment in that industry. However, there was no detailed manpower planning, in which the occupational and skill needs of an industry were matched with the skills produced by the educational and training system. While some individuals in the Ministry of Labor have indicated an interest in manpower planning, there is no major force within the government pushing for such planning.

In summary, Spain has been relatively successful in obtaining rapid economic growth over the past ten or so years, due largely to foreign investments, expanding markets, and tourism. Whether economic planning made a significant contribution to these economic gains is debatable. Manpower and education were not parts of Spain's economic planning. As industry expanded, demand for skilled manpower increased. The education and training institutions increased their output, but the numbers and the mix were never quite right. Moonlighting is a common phenomenon for white-collar and skilled blue-collar workers; at the same time unemployment rates, especially among the unskilled and poorly trained are rather high. There seems to be a growing interest in manpower and education planning, but so far, relatively little has been done in these areas of planning.

Conclusion and Policy Implications

Spain's authoritarian-type government has set the economic scene, with the nation's prime focus on economic growth and integration with the Common Market. Minimum concessions were to be made in social and political matters, only enough to assuage the concerns of the western European nations about Franco's dictatorship.

Various economic policies were adopted to attain rapid growth, and economic planning was part of the coordinated effort. The nation's Planning Commission followed, in general, the indicative planning techniques of France, although it formulated rather specific and directed plans for the different divisions of the public sector. Spain's industrial growth has been substantial. However, there are serious doubts that these gains were the results of Spain's economic plans; in some instances, especially in the public sector, it is clear that the policies and programs called for by the plans were disregarded. While the Planning Commission had the responsibility of drafting the plans, the specific programs were in the hands of various ministries, such as the Ministry of Education and the Ministry of Agriculture, and the ministries did not always agree with the Planning Commission on policies and programs.

The staff of the Planning Commission indicated that neither in Plan I nor in Plan II did the Commission feel that manpower was an important factor in economic planning. This conclusion was based on the assumption that at early stages of economic growth there is no need for manpower planning since any and all skills are needed by growing industries. Only at some later stage of industrialization do shortages start developing; and it is at that point that manpower planning may become important. Despite this lack of concern with manpower by the Planning Commission, other government agencies did show an interest, although they lacked authority to engage in manpower planning.

In the early 1960's the OECD's Directorate of Scientific Affairs undertook a series of studies in the Mediterranean area, entitled *The Mediterranean Regional Project,* and one study was on education and manpower in Spain. Using broad occupational categories the study developed projections and targets, and it did propose educational and manpower planning.

That the Planning Commission misjudged the need for manpower planning is indicated by a number of factors. The increasing amount of moonlighting by both white-collar workers and skilled blue-collar workers implies a shortage of such skills. There is sufficient evidence to conclude that Spain has a shortage of (1) various master craftsmen and foremen, especially auto mechanics and electricians, (2) technicians and intermediate technologists, (3) teachers for all educational levels, and especially in science and technical subjects, (4) various administrative specialists, and (5) new skills and professions for such modern industries as communications and electronic data processing. While official statistics indicate that unemployment is low, there is evidence that the unemployment rate is greater than the official rate. In addition, net emigration has relieved the pressure on the labor market, a pressure which could have caused considerable disturbance to the rapid economic growth. Many of the emigrants did return to Spain, after gaining experience as industrial workers in some of the more modern plants and industries in Western Europe, but relatively few of the returnees found jobs in which they could use their newly acquired skills.

Failing to include manpower in the economic planning process meant that the Planning Commission left to others the whole thrust of changing the educational and training systems of the nation. The Ministry of Education developed a plan to restructure the education system, and the plan has many commendable aspects. However, it is not tied in with skill needs of the growing sectors of economy, and the traditional skills will continue to be taught with the same traditional programs. And even where innovations in the educational process are made, they are not likely to mesh with the plans developed by the Planning Commission. Thus, despite its authoritarian government and highly centralized power structure, Spain shows many weaknesses in its planning efforts, weaknesses that are more common in democratic-capitalistic nations.

The government and its Planning Commission fail to recognize that Spain has already arrived at a stage of growth where manpower bottlenecks are hindering future growth. Firms and industries are tailoring their technology to available manpower, rather than introducing more modern equipment and facilities which would require sophisticated skills not readily available in the Spanish labor markets. Such losses in productivity can be critical for future economic growth. In the meantime, distortions in the labor market are occurring, with workers unemployed because of lack of training or of misdirected training, and with workers underemployed considerably below their capacity. Such wastage of human resources is a loss to national income, which Spain can ill afford at this stage of her growth.

The Planning Commission of Spain should engage in manpower and educational planning along with economic planning, and these various planning aspects should be coordinated into a single, harmonious plan. Indicative planning for the private sector may be wise, if Spain is to foster an open, market economy. However, in the public sector the Planning Commission should have the responsibility to assure that other ministries and government organizations carry through the policies and programs developed in the plan.

It makes little sense to permit, through a lack of planning, manpower bottlenecks to hinder the economic growth and modernization of Spain. With manpower planning for industries' needs, in terms of skill and education levels, many of the major manpower problems could be avoided. And as Spain reaches higher levels of industrialization, with even still greater needs for highly specialized manpower, the possibilities of mismatching the supply and demand of manpower are greater. Manpower and education planning at this stage of growth can save Spain considerable grief in the near future.

Appendix Tables

TABLE III-1

Average Hourly Earnings in Selected Industries, First Quarter 1967, 1968, 1969

Selected Industries	First Quarter 1967, (average) Pesetas	First Quarter 1967, (average) Dollars	First Quarter 1968, (average) Pesetas	First Quarter 1968, (average) Dollars	First Quarter 1969 Average Pesetas	First Quarter 1969 Average Dollars	First Quarter 1969 Skilled Male Pesetas	First Quarter 1969 Unskilled Male Pesetas	Percent differential between skilled and unskilled
Coal mining	41.64	.59	48.16	.69	52.81	.75	65.95	38.69	70
Food, drink and tobacco	23.10	.33	25.89	.37	28.57	.41	35.21	22.70	55
Shoes, clothing and leather	18.05	.26	19.37	.28	21.84	.31	29.69	21.14	40
Printing and publishing	30.40	.43	31.67	.45	36.53	.52	44.53	24.46	82
Chemical products	27.16	.39	30.61	.44	32.89	.47	35.84	24.69	45
Construction	20.69	.30	22.80	.32	24.57	.35	29.99	19.17	56
Commerce	23.76	.34	26.46	.38	29.44	.42	31.03	22.59	38
Banking	46.28	.66	56.80	.81	60.40	.86	67.18	40.71	65

Source: Instituto Nacional de Estadística, *Salarios, primer trimestre, Año 1969* (Madrid 1969), *passim*.
Note: Dollar figures were calculated by converting the pesetas at the official exchange rate of 70 pesetas to the dollar.

TABLE III-2

EMPLOYMENT BY ECONOMIC ACTIVITIES, 1966 AND FORECAST FOR 1971
(in thousands)

Economic Activities	1966		1971		Difference 1966—1971	
	Number	Percent Distribution	Number	Percent Distribution	Absolute	Percent
Agriculture	3,506.6	28.7	3,023.5	23.3	-483.1	-13.78
Fishing	200.0	1.6	208.5	1.6	8.5	4.25
Mining	163.7	1.3	123.7	1.0	-40.0	-24.43
Food Manufacturers	594.4	4.9	714.4	5.5	120.0	20.19
Shoes & clothing	683.1	5.6	671.1	5.2	-12.0	-1.76
Wood and paper	404.1	3.3	454.1	3.5	50.0	12.37
Chemicals	203.1	1.7	226.1	1.7	23.0	11.32
Non-metallic mfg	205.0	1.7	219.0	1.7	14.0	6.83
Metal mfg	1,049.7	8.6	1,246.2	9.6	196.5	18.72
Construction	985.5	8.1	1,190.1	9.2	204.6	20.76
Water and Energy	100.2	0.8	106.2	0.8	6.0	5.99
Commerce	1,325.1	10.8	1,682.1	13.0	357.0	26.94
Transport	609.6	5.0	656.2	5.1	46.6	7.64
Other Services	2,183.6	17.9	2,451.6	18.8	268.0	12.27
TOTAL Employment	12,213.7	100.0	12,972.8	100.0	759.1	6.22
Unemployment	189.0		237.8		48.8	25.82
TOTAL Labor Force	12,402.7		13,210.6		807.9	6.51

Source: Report of Ponencia de Trabajo to Planning Commission (unpublished), p. 25.

TABLE III-3

LABOR FORCE BY SOCIOECONOMIC GROUPS, 1964-1968
(in thousands)

Socioeconomic Groups	1964 Number	1964 Percent	1968 Number	1968 Percent	Change 1964 to 1968 Absolute	Change 1964 to 1968 Percent
TOTAL	11,707.6	100.0	12,277.3	100.0	569.7	4.87
Agriculture employers	89.7	.77	61.9	.50	-27.8	-30.99
Farmers without workers	2,656.0	22.69	2,666.0	21.71	10.0	.38
Members of farm coops	6.9	.06	5.1	.04	-1.8	-26.09
Farm workers	1,169.2	9.99	1,069.8	8.71	-99.4	-8.50
Nonfarm employers of large & medium firms	118.7	1.01	130.0	1.06	11.3	9.52
Nonfarm employers of small firms	187.5	1.60	215.4	1.75	27.9	14.88
Nonfarm entrepreneurs without workers	1,290.0	11.02	1,427.7	11.63	137.7	10.67
University-level professions	70.3	.60	50.2	.41	-20.1	-28.59
Members of nonfarm coops	4.0	.03	3.1	.03	-.9	-22.50
Managers of firms and businesses	19.7	.17	15.4	.13	-4.3	-21.83
High level employees[1]	93.6	.80	112.3	.91	18.7	19.98
Medium level employees[2]	1,437.9	12.28	1,741.2	14.18	303.3	21.09
Skilled workers	2,644.2	22.59	2,971.0	24.20	326.8	12.36
Unskilled & semiskilled workers	1,171.5	10.01	1,040.1	8.47	-131.4	-11.22
Service workers	665.6	5.69	722.3	5.88	56.7	8.52
Others	82.8	.71	45.8	.37	-37.0	-44.69

1. Includes those in high level managerial and administrative positions, and other salaried positions which require some post-secondary school education.
2. Includes technicians, office workers, salesmen of all types, and other white collar employees.
Source: Instituto Nacional de Estadística, Población activa en 1968 (Madrid, 1969), p. 44; and Población Activa en 1964 (Madrid, 1965), p. 134.

TABLE III-4

LABOR FORCE BY PROFESSIONAL STATUS AND AGE GROUPS, 1968
(in thousands)

Professional Status \ Age Groups	Total	14 years of age	15 to 19 years	20 to 24 years	25 to 44 years	45 to 64 years	65 years and over
TOTAL	12,277.3	106.2	1,435.8	1,518.7	4,546.7	4,106.5	563.4
Employer	323.9	—	—	3.2	126.9	158.0	35.8
Entrepreneur without employees	2,542.0	—	6.2	65.9	861.7	1,304.9	303.3
Self-employed workers	150.6	—	8.3	20.6	56.2	55.7	9.8
Family help	1,609.1	34.8	357.3	304.3	544.8	316.3	51.6
Employees	7,510.3	65.9	1,030.8	1,102.9	2,917.5	2,233.4	159.8
Private sector	6,717.4	65.7	1,011.1	1,044.2	2,618.5	1,844.9	133.0
Public sector	792.9	0.2	19.7	58.7	299.0	388.5	26.8
Unemployed	134.2	5.5	32.0	21.5	37.5	35.7	2.0
Others	7.2	—	1.2	0.3	2.1	2.5	1.1

Source: Instituto Nacional de Estadística, Población activa en 1968, (Madrid, 1969), p. 51.

TABLE III-5

LABOR FORCE BY PROFESSIONAL STATUS AND HOURS WORKED PER WEEK
(in thousands), 1968

Professional Status	Total	Number of Persons Who Have Worked								
		0 hours	1 to 14 hours	15 to 29 hours	30 to 39 hours	40 to 44 hours	45 to 48 hours	49 to 54 hours	55 to 59 hours	60 hours and more
TOTAL	12,277.3	500.4	59.4	278.3	540.0	870.8	5,690.3	2,203.2	356.4	1,778.5
Employer	323.9	4.0	1.4	7.6	10.7	16.0	110.5	83.7	11.3	78.7
Entrepreneur without employees	2,542.0	32.2	16.3	80.4	132.9	99.8	700.1	713.9	124.3	642.1
Self-employed workers	150.6	3.9	1.9	8.8	14.9	7.7	55.3	30.3	5.1	22.7
Family help	1,609.1	54.1	11.0	48.5	86.7	59.6	455.5	401.3	88.2	404.2
Employees	7,510.3	270.0	28.7	132.4	294.1	687.6	4,367.3	972.5	127.4	630.3
Private sector	6,717.4	251.8	25.9	105.5	176.2	606.8	3,920.5	932.5	118.0	580.2
Public sector	792.9	18.2	2.8	26.9	117.9	80.8	446.8	40.0	9.4	50.1
Unemployed	134.2	134.2	—	—	—	—	—	—	—	—
Other	7.2	2.0	0.1	0.6	0.7	0.1	1.6	1.5	0.1	0.5

Source: Instituto Nacional de Estadística, *Población activa en 1968* (Madrid, 1969), p. 53.

TABLE IV-1
LABOR FORCE BY SOCIOECONOMIC GROUPS AND CULTURAL LEVEL, 1968
(in thousands)

Socioeconomic Groups	TOTAL	Literate Persons				Illiterates
		Completed Special Studies			Did not complete special studies	
		with University degree	with secondary school degree	without a degree		
TOTAL	12,277.3	186.5	464.0	493.6	10,622.4	510.8
Agricultural employers	61.9	1.9	3.6	3.1	53.3	—
Farmers without workers	2,666.0	4.4	4.9	15.4	2,499.9	141.4
Members of farm crops	5.1	0.2	0.2	0.1	4.4	0.2
Farm laborers	1,069.8	—	0.8	9.6	898.3	161.1
Nonfarm employers of large and medium firms	130.0	7.1	16.0	14.0	92.9	—
Nonfarm employers of small firms	215.4	7.0	8.7	16.2	182.8	0.7
Nonfarm entrepreneurs without workers	1,427.7	15.9	24.9	57.0	1,298.7	31.2
Professionals & related	50.2	36.2	7.4	1.0	5.6	—
Members of nonfarm coops	3.1	—	—	—	2.9	0.2
Managers of firms	15.4	3.2	4.3	2.1	5.8	—
High level employees	112.3	83.0	5.2	3.1	21.0	—
Medium level employees[1]	1,741.2	23.2	360.7	229.6	1,116.8	10.9
Skilled workers	2,971.0	3.1	22.9	101.9	2,809.7	33.4
Unskilled & semiskilled	1,040.1	—	0.8	17.2	955.2	66.9
Service Workers	722.3	—	1.4	19.6	637.9	63.4
Others	45.8	1.3	2.2	3.7	37.2	1.4

1. Includes technicians, office workers, salesmen of all types, and other white collar employees.
Source: Instituto Nacional de Estadística, *Población activa en 1968* (Madrid, 1969), p. 64

TABLE IV-2

PERCENT DISTRIBUTION OF LABOR FORCE BY SEX AND AGE GROUPS, 1968

Sex	Total		14 years of age	15 to 19	20 to 24	25 to 44	45 to 64	65 and over
	Number in thousands	Percent						
Total	12,277.3	100.0	.87	11.69	12.37	37.03	33.45	4.59
Male	9,359.5	100.0	.79	9.69	10.68	39.03	35.26	4.54
Female	2,917.8	100.0	1.10	18.11	17.79	30.62	27.64	4.74
Total	12,277.3	100.0	100.0	100.0	100.0	100.0	100.0	100.0
Male	9,359.5	76.23	69.87	63.20	65.82	80.35	80.36	75.45
Female	2,917.8	23.77	30.13	36.80	34.18	19.65	19.64	24.55

Source: Instituto Nacional de Estadística, *Población activa en 1968* (Madrid, 1969), p. 51.

TABLE V-1

NUMBER OF STUDENTS PER 1000 INHABITANTS AND
PERCENTAGE DISTRIBUTION OF ENROLLMENTS BY LEVEL OF EDUCATION
FOR SELECTED COUNTRIES

Country and Year		Number of Students per 1000 Inhabitants	Percentage Distribution of Total Enrollments by Levels of Schooling		
			Primary Level	Secondary Level	Higher Level
Spain	1966	171	73	24	3
West Germany	1964	185	62	36	2
France	1964	224	67	29	4
Italy	1964	177	63	34	3
Great Britain	1964	225	50	48	2

Source: UNESCO statistics, as quoted in Ministerio de Educación y Ciencias, *La educación en España*, pp. 36-37.

TABLE V-2

PUBLIC EXPENDITURES ON EDUCATION
FOR SELECTED COUNTRIES, 1968

Country	Public Expenditure on Education	
	As Percent of GNP	As Percent of Total Public Expenditure
Spain	1.8	11.7
Italy	4.8	19.8
Belgium	5.0	—
France	4.4	19.1
Germany	3.6	10.9
Sweden	7.9	26.9
Switzerland	4.1	19.3

Source: United Nations, *Statistical Yearbook 1970* (N.Y., 1971), pp. 778-781.

TABLE V-3

PREPRIMARY AND PRIMARY SCHOOL ENROLLMENTS, AND STUDENTS PER TEACHER, 1954-55 THROUGH 1967-68

Year	Total Enrollment in thousands	Index 1954-55= 100.0	Percent Enrollment in Public Schools	Percent Enrollment in Private Schools	No. of Students Per Teacher in All Schools	No. of Students Per Teacher in Public Schools	No. of Students Per Teacher in Private Schools
1954-55	3,373.9	100.0	76.3	23.7	40	42	35
1955-56	3,454.6	102.4	76.6	23.4	40	42	35
1956-57	3,248.0	96.3	74.6	25.4	37	37	37
1957-58	3,309.5	98.1	73.9	26.1	36	36	38
1958-59	3,335.0	98.8	73.9	26.1	36	34	43
1959-60	3,370.4	99.9	73.8	26.2	36	34	43
1960-61	3,387.4	100.4	73.9	26.1	35	33	43
1961-62	3,409.7	101.1	74.0	26.0	35	33	42
1962-63	3,452.7	102.3	73.7	26.3	35	33	43
1963-64	3,505.4	103.9	73.4	26.6	35	33	41
1964-65	3,762.7	111.5	72.2	27.8	35	33	40
1965-66	3,942.2	116.8	70.6	29.4	35	33	40
1966-67	4,025.2	119.3	69.5	30.5	34	33	39
1967-68	4,178.7	123.9	69.3	30.7	34	32	38

Source: Comisaría del Plan. *Enseñanza y formación profesional* (Madrid, 1967), pp. 24-27.

143

TABLE V-4

STUDENTS IN THE GENERAL BACCALAUREATE PROGRAMS, BY LEVEL OF PROGRAM, 1958-59 THROUGH 1967-68

Year	Total		Lower		Higher		Pre-University	
	Number	Index 1958-59 = 100	Number	Index 1958-59 = 100	Number	Index 1958-59 = 100	Number	Index 1958-59 = 100
1958-59	420,852	100.0	353,186	100.0	51,583	100.0	16,083	100.0
1959-60	448,311	106.52	376,712	106.66	54,557	105.76	17,042	105.96
1960-61	474,057	112.64	394,629	111.73	60,207	116.71	19,221	119.51
1961-62	564,111	134.04	469,737	132.99	74,008	143.47	20,366	126.63
1962-63	622,872	148.00	517,849	146.62	82,023	159.01	23,000	143.00
1963-64	682,226	162.10	566,736	160.46	89,396	173.30	26,094	162.24
1964-65	745,044	177.03	622,616	176.28	95,388	184.92	27,040	168.12
1965-66	834,290	198.23	697,292	197.42	108,891	211.09	28.107	174.76
1966-67	929,589	220.88	775,929	219.69	123,576	239.56	30,084	187.05
1967-68	1,119,803	266.07	930,313	263.40	154,945	300.37	34,545	214.79

Source: Ministerio de Educación, *Datos y cifros de la enseñanza en España, 1969*, p. 45.

TABLE V-5

Students Who Enrolled for Final Exams and Who Passed, at Different Levels of General Baccalaureate Programs 1958-59 through 1967-68

Year	Lower Level Baccalaureate			Higher Level Baccalaureate			Pre-University Level		
	Students Enrolled for Exam	Students Passed	Percent Passed	Students Enrolled for Exam	Students Passed	Percent Passed	Students Enrolled for Exam	Students Passed	Percent Passed
1958-59	89,032	44,258	49.7	35,667	20,519	57.5	22,688	12,888	56.8
1959-60	100,328	53,751	53.6	35,853	22,526	62.8	29,948	11,793	43.8
1960-61	108,693	59,371	54.6	36,672	23,570	64.3	20,783	13,505	45.3
1961-62	120,545	67,071	55.6	43,358	26,918	62.1	31,666	14,349	45.3
1962-63	124,529	62,058	49.8	46,138	29,217	63.3	37,257	18,410	49.4
1963-64	136,906	71,108	51.9	46,050	28,213	61.3	38,680	15,708	40.6
1964-65	152,161	76,850	50.5	49,663	31,521	63.5	47,453	20,337	42.8
1965-66	157,112	78,956	50.3	53,994	30,737	56.9	51,060	21,741	42.5
1966-67	189,357	95,549	50.4	66,424	35,702	53.7	53,549	23,506	43.9
1967-68	219,254	98,056	44.7	82,570	44,479	53.9	—	—	—

Source: Ministerio de Educación, *La educación en España*, p. 65; for the years 1966-67 and 1967-68 data were computed from Ministerio de Educación, *Datos y cifras de la enseñanza en España 1969*, p. 47.

TABLE V-6

Enrollment in Technical Baccalaureate Programs by Area of Study, 1959-60 through 1966-67

Year	Total		Agriculture Husbandry		Industry Mining		Maritime Fishing		Administration	
	Number	Percent	Number	Percent	Number	Percent	Number	Percent	Number	Percent
1959-60	14,287	100.0	7,434	52.03	4,370	30.59	1,092	7.64	1,391	9.74
1960-61	23,378	100.0	9,462	40.47	5,376	23.00	1,064	4.55	7,476	31.98
1961-62	29,474	100.0	11,416	38.73	5,542	18.80	1,229	4.17	11,287	38.30
1962-63	30,396	100.0	11,880	39.08	6,823	22.45	1,070	3.52	10,623	34.95
1963-64	36,253	100.0	13,996	38.61	7,153	19.73	1,214	3.35	13,290	38.31
1964-65	44,482	100.0	15,199	34.17	10,380	23.34	1,234	2.77	17,669	39.72
1965-66	49,796	100.0	16,255	32.64	11,476	23.05	1,284	2.58	20,781	41.73
1966-67	55,221	100.0	18,434	33.38	13,769	24.93	1,554	2.81	21,464	38.86

Source: Comisaría del Plan, *Enseñanza y formación profesional*, p. 46.

TABLE V-7

NUMBER OF STUDENTS AND PROFESSORS IN STATE AND NON-STATE NORMAL SCHOOLS, 1957-58 through 1967-68

Year	Number of Students			Number of Professors			Number of Students per Professor		
	Total	In State Schools	In Non-State Schools	Total	In State Schools	In Non-State Schools	Total	In State Schools	In Non-State Schools
1957-58	39,084	34,824	4,260	2,303	1,615	688	17.0	21.6	6.2
1958-59	40,359	35,800	4,559	2,418	1,660	758	16.7	21.6	6.0
1959-60	41,573	36,470	5,103	2,508	1,714	794	16.6	21.3	6.4
1960-61	43,126	37,626	5,500	2,450	1,685	765	17.6	22.3	7.2
1961-62	43,106	37,435	5,668	2,529	1,673	856	17.0	22.4	6.6
1962-63	45,898	39,052	6,846	2,816	1,501	1,315	16.3	26.0	5.2
1963-64	50,363	41,913	8,450	2,538	1,161	1,377	19.8	36.1	6.1
1964-65	58,310	48,232	10,078	2,386	1,028	1,358	24.4	46.9	7.4
1965-66	63,116	53,483	9,633	2,429	1,088	1,341	26.0	49.1	7.2
1966-67	68,972	56,891	12,081	2,638	1,064	1,574	26.1	53.5	7.7
1967-68	69,110	62,182	6,928	2,548	1,152	1,496	27.1	54.0	4.6

Source: Ministerio de Educación, *Datos y cifras de la enseñanza en España, 1969*, Tomo 1, pp. 64-66.

TABLE V-8

Enrollments in Industrial Programs of Vocational Education,[1] by Levels of Training, 1960-61 through 1966-67

Year	Total Enrollment		Students Enrolled in						Students Who Completed Studies in	
			Pre-Apprentice Level		Apprentice Level		Craftsman Level		Apprenticeship Level	Craftsman Level
	Number	Percent	Number	Percent	Number	Percent	Number	Percent		
1960-61	65,429	100.0	17,308	26.4	45,000	68.7	3,121	4.7	—	—
1961-62	76,529	100.0	20,183	26.3	51,472	67.2	4,871	6.3	—	—
1962-63	84,570	100.0	22,243	26.3	56,356	66.6	5,971	7.0	—	—
1963-64	95,862	100.0	24,900	25.9	64,065	66.8	6,897	7.1	9,506	2,295
1964-65	111,262	100.0	29,548	26.5	73,125	65.7	8,589	7.7	11,373	1,484
1965-66	125,080	100.0	31,763	25.3	81,940	65.5	11,377	9.0	17,053	4,698
1966-67	130,973	100.0	32,569	24.8	85,969	65.6	12,435	9.4	14,748	4,791

1. These figures do not include enrollments in military schools.
Source: INE, *Estadística de la enseñanza media en España*, II, Curso 1966-67, pp. 110-111.

TABLE V-9

UNIVERSITY ENROLLMENTS BY SPECIALTY
1956-57 THROUGH 1967-68

Year	Total		Science	Political Science and Economics	Pharmacy	Law	Philosophy and Letters	Medicine	Veterinary Science
	Number	Index 1956-57=100							
1956-57	62,215	100.0	8,154	3,290	7,574	19,471	5,890	15,621	2,215
1957-58	64,281	103.3	10,397	4,082	7,303	17,847	6,486	16,592	1,574
1958-59	62,985	101.2	10,679	5,104	7,303	15,724	6,853	16,110	1,212
1959-60	63,786	102.5	12,552	5,742	6,512	14,773	7,345	15,989	874
1960-61	62,105	99.8	13,071	6,365	5,068	13,673	8,648	14,470	810
1961-62	64,010	102.8	13,290	7,034	4,978	13,438	9,554	15,117	599
1962-63	69,377	111.5	14,869	8,200	4,982	13,418	10,624	16,758	526
1963-64	80,074	128.7	17,788	10,356	4,789	14,103	12,433	20,099	506
1964-65	85,148	136.8	19,489	11,087	4,685	14,750	14,837	19,769	531
1965-66	92,983	149.4	19,545	11,950	5,421	15,307	17,359	22,851	550
1966-67	105,370	169.3	22,019	16,850	5,707	16,241	20,189	23,723	641
1967-68	115,590	185.8	25,596	18,657	5,545	16,574	24,510	23,940	768

Source: Comisaría del Plan. *Enseñanza y formación profesional*, p. 85.
For 1967-68 data: INE, *Estadística de la enseñanza superior en España*, Curso 1967-70, p. 17.

TABLE V-10

Number of University Students Who Completed their Studies, by Specialty, 1956-57 through 1967-68

Year	Total		Science	Political Science and Economics	Law	Pharmacy	Philosphy and Letters	Medicine	Veterinary Science
	Number	Index 1956-57= 100.0							
1956-57	5,294	100.0	783	46	1,754	408	689	1,238	376
1957-58	5,016	94.7	475	96	1,672	502	759	1,251	261
1958-59	4,721	89.2	565	99	1,448	453	677	1,251	228
1959-60	5,078	95.9	478	138	1,509	483	742	1,495	233
1960-61	4,475	84.5	536	188	1,285	396	828	1,104	138
1961-62	4,949	93.5	642	189	1,314	312	774	1,600	118
1962-63	4,632	87.5	680	176	1,160	269	859	1,393	95
1963-64	5,341	100.9	622	334	1,079	518	1,209	1,504	75
1964-65	5,796	109.5	1,161	345	1,116	514	1,018	1,607	85
1965-66	6,028	113.9	1,005	502	1,161	539	1,054	1,725	42
1966-67	6,924	130.8	1,190	378	1,215	573	1,775	1,751	42
1967-68	8,280	156.4	1,346	827	1,454	622	1,930	2,043	58

Source: Comisaría del Plan, *Enseñanza y formación profesional*, p. 89.
   For 1967-68 data: INE. *Estadística de la enseñanza superior en España*, Curso 1967-68, p. 17.

TABLE V-11

ENROLLMENTS IN ENGINEERING INSTITUTES BY
SPECIALTY, 1956-57 THROUGH 1967-68

Year	Total		Architecture	Aeronautics	Agronomy	Highways	Industry	Mines	Mountains	Naval	Telecommunication
	Number	Index 1956-57=100									
1956-57	4,744	100.0	602	174	338	388	2,375	258	222	182	205
1957-58	5,393	113.7	519	188	371	421	2,913	385	252	126	218
1958-59	4,901	103.3	505	201	385	435	2,359	381	248	129	258
1959-60	6,803	143.4	663	255	477	504	3,724	444	244	163	326
1960-61	7,239	152.6	642	311	675	439	3,644	505	233	200	296
1961-62[1]	18,321	386.2	1,779	697	1,577	2,009	9,384	1,021	452	551	851
1962-63	18,975	400.0	1,903	649	1,488	1,980	10,092	1,078	466	477	842
1963-64	22,781	480.2	2,390	754	2,043	2,338	11,680	1,378	559	643	996
1964-65	27,499	579.6	4,205	896	2,006	2,676	13,799	1,420	533	775	1,189
1965-66	32,896	693.4	6,066	1,113	3,157	2,897	14,733	1,626	671	902	1,731
1966-67	36,038	759.6	6,855	1,329	3,178	3,658	15,362	1,395	625	1,056	2,580
1967-68	38,695	815.7	8,158	1,294	3,290	4,969	15,272	1,328	556	1,156	2,672

1. Change in definition in this year.
Source: Comisaría del Plan, *Enseñanza y formación profesional*, p. 88.
For 1967-68 data: INE, *Estadística de la enseñanza superior en España*, Curso 1967-68, p. 37.

TABLE V-12

NUMBER OF STUDENTS OF ENGINEERING INSTITUTES WHO COMPLETED THEIR STUDIES, BY SPECIALTY, 1956-57 THROUGH 1967-68

Year	Total		Architec-ture	Aeron-autics	Agron-omy	Highways	Indus-try	Mines	Mountains	Naval	Telecom-munication
	Number	Index 1956-57= 100									
1956-57	637	100.0	122	25	42	62	270	56	20	25	15
1957-58	709	111.3	84	29	45	87	298	58	48	31	29
1958-59	758	119.0	98	31	56	80	345	56	43	22	27
1959-60	778	122.1	84	32	64	68	370	62	46	22	30
1960-61	813	127.6	93	32	63	79	374	67	40	19	39
1961-62	924	145.0	88	38	78	84	461	68	38	31	38
1962-63	1,214	190.6	81	20	81	69	774	67	44	38	40
1963-64	1,270	199.4	145	57	159	167	476	67	51	48	100
1964-65	1,638	257.1	180	60	249	105	790	97	50	39	68
1965-66	1,539	241.6	191	66	106	157	785	83	26	49	66
1966-67	1,312	206.0	153	42	139	44	673	85	36	42	96
1967-68	1,587	249.1	246	66	79	147	737	111	46	55	100

Source: Comisaría del Plan, *Enseñanza y formación profesional*, p. 90.
For 1967-68 data: INE, *Estadística de la enseñanza superior en España, Curso 1967-68*, p. 37.

152

TABLE VI-1

"Free" Students as a Percentage of Total
Enrollments, by Faculty, for Selected Years

Faculty	Academic Year 1960-61	Academic Year 1963-64	Academic Year 1967-68
Medicine	26%	28%	10%
Pharmacy	45	38	12
Veterinary Science	61	48	28
Law	51	41	30
Philosophy & Letters	37	33	24
Science	15	19	14
Economics	60	58	36
All Universities	32	34	20
All Technological Institutes	7	18	22

Source: Fundacion FOESSA, *op. cit.*, Table 14.70.

153

NOTES

Notes to Chapter I

1. Frederick Harbison and Charles A. Myers, *Education, Manpower and Economic Growth* (New York: McGraw-Hill Book Co., 1964), p. 2.
2. United Nations, *Statistical Yearbook*, 1969.
3. Fundación FOESSA, *Informe sociológico sobre la situacion social de España 1970* (Editorial Euramérica, SA., 1970), p. 148.
4. *Ibid.*, p. 520.
5. Organizacion Sindical, Vicesecretaria, Nacional de Ordinacion Económica, *Evolución Socioeconómica de España 1968*, (Madred 1969), p. 6.
6. Fundación FOESSA, *op. cit.*, p. 576.
7. *Ya* (Madrid), August 5, 1970.
8. Fundación FOESSA, *Supplemento al sociológico sobre la situación social de España 1970*, (No. 1, Enero-Marzo 1971), p. 16.
9. Fundación FOESSA, *Informe*, p. 561.
10. *Ibid.*, pp. 566-567.
11. See, for example, International Bank, *Economic Development of Spain* (1963), and Banco de Bilbao, *Informe económica, 1963* (Madrid, 1964).
12. International Bank, *op. cit.*, pp. 330-331.
13. Banco de Bilbao, *op. cit.*, p. 201.
14. Organization for Economic Cooperation and Development (OECD), *Technical Assistance and the Economic Development of Spain* (Paris, 1968), pp. 21-23.
15. U.S. Department of Commerce, Bureau of International Commerce, *Country Market Survey: Spain*, (U.S. Government Printing Office, August, 1970), p. 27.
16. Report by INI, as cited by the newspaper, *LaVanguardia Española*, June 13, 1970.
17. Fundación FOESSA, *op. cit.*, pp. 1056-1057.
18. *Ibid.*, p. 1120.
19. *Ibid.*, p. 363.
20. Stanley G. Payne, *Franco's Spain* (New York: Thomas Y. Crowell Co., 1967), p. 78.
21. The literal meaning of the Spanish work "enchufe" is an electrical plug or connection, but it is commonly used to denote personal connections, whether social or family with someone of importance.

Notes to Chapter II

1. Eric N. Baklanoff, "Spain and the Atlantic Community: A Study of the Incipient Integration and Economic Development," *Economic Development and Cultural Change*, Vol. 16, No. 4. 1968, pp. 589-590.
2. George Hills, *Spain* (New York: Praeger Publishers, 1970), pp. 245-246.
3. International Bank for Reconstruction and Development, *The Economic Development of Spain* (Baltimore: Johns Hopkins Press, 1963), p. 45.
4. Charles W. Anderson, *The Political Economy of Modern Spain* (Madison: University of Wisconsin Press, 1970), p. 47.
5. Ramón Tamames, *Introducción a la economía Española*, (Madrid: Alianza Editorial, 1967), p. 350.
6. Anderson, *op. cit.*, pp. 39 and 46.
7. Antonio Robert, *Perspectivas de la economía Española*, p. 106, as quoted in Anderson, *op. cit.*, p. 28.
8. IBRD, *op. cit.*, p. 45.
9. *Ibid.*, p. 46.
10. International Labour Office, *The Labour and Trade Union Situation in Spain* (Geneva, 1969), p. 29.
11. Banco de Bilbao, *Informe Anual 1963*, p. 238.
12. Stephen Clissold, *Spain* (New York: Walker & Co., 1969), p. 181.
13. International Labour Office, *op. cit.*, p. 275.
14. In order to broaden his political base to include right-wing groups and individuals who were not Falangists, but not to permit other political parties, Franco established El Movimiento (the Movement) as the only legal party. While the Movement incorporates the Falangists and many non-Falangists, there was little differentiation made in the press (even when tightly regulated). The leaders of the Falange became the leaders of the Movement, and in most cases the press referred to the Falange as the official party of Spain. From a purely organized power basis, it is the Falange that has significance, and therefore this study will use Falange rather than the Movement.
15. *New York Times*, November 27, 1969.
16. International Labour Office, *op. cit.*, p. 30.
17. *New York Times*, November 27, 1969. See also *Newsweek*, July 8, 1968, p. 32.
18. Each major industry had its own sindicato, and by law not only did all workers have to be members but also all members of management. Although they bear some of the trappings of unions, the sindicatos lack the basic elements of free trade unions.
19. Clissold, *op. cit.*, p. 120.
20. I.L.O., *op. cit.*, p. 278.
21. *New York Times*, November 27, 1969.
22. *International Herald Tribune*, June 20-21, 1971.
23. *Ibid.*, May 27, 1970. See also, *Ya* (Madrid), May 28, 1970.
24. *International Herald Tribune*, June 20-21, 1970.
25. *Ya* (Madrid), June 26, 1970.
26. Clissold, *op. cit.*, p. 122.
27. Baklanoff, *loc. cit.*, p. 590.
28. International Labour Office, *op. cit.*, p. 31.
29. *Ibid.*
30. IBRD, *op. cit.*, p. 46.
31. OEEC, *Tercer informe sobre la economía española* (Madrid: Oficina de Coordinación y Programación Económica, 1961), pp. 10-11.
32. *Ibid.*, p. 50.
33. IBRD, *op. cit.*, pp. 46-47.
34. Anderson, *op. cit.*, pp. 155-156.
35. Computed from statistics in Banco de Bilbao, *Informe económica 1968* (Madrid, 1969), p. 310.

36. Published as *Plan de desarrollo económico y social para el período 1964-1967* (Madrid, 1963).

37. International Labour Office, *op. cit.*, p. 32.

38. Anderson, *op. cit.*, p. 204.

39. *Ibid.*, pp. 7, 10-11.

40. Organizacion Sindical, 'Vicesecretaría Nacional de Ordenación Económica, *Evolución socioeconómica de España 1968*, (Madrid, 1969), p. 90.

41. As quoted in *Plan de desarrollo económica y social para el período 1964-1967, p. 1.*

42. *Ibid.*, pp. 25-26.

43. Speech given by López Rodó before the Cortes on February 7, 1969, as quoted in Comisaría del Plan de Desarrollo Económico y Social, *Hoha Informativa 169*, (Madrid: Enero-Abril, 1969), p. 7.

44. Ramón Tamames, *España ante un segundo plan de desarrollo*, (Barcelona: Editorial Nova Terra, 1968), pp. 70, 90-91.

45. *Ibid.*, p. 172.

46. Organización Sindical, *op. cit.*, pp. 91-92.

47. Article by López Rodó in *Financial Times*, as quoted in Comisaría del Plan de Desarrollo Económico y Social, *Hoja Informativa 269*, p. 106.

48. The secretariat of the Board of Labor did prepare a report, but while the Planning Commission published the report of all other Boards and Committees, it did not publish one for the Board of Labor. The office response by the Planning Commission was that the report was forthcoming. Informally, the author was told that the members of the Board could not agree on a number of significant factors. The author did see a copy of a draft of the report.

49. In personal interviews with Dr. Javier Irastorza, the Director of Research of the Planning Commission, and with staff members of the Commission, it was made clear to me that in neither Plan I nor Plan II did the Commission feel that manpower was an important factor in economic planning. It was argued that perhaps at some later state in development of Spain manpower planning may become important.

Notes to Chapter III

1. Fundación FOESSA, *op. cit.*, 1966, Table 6.7.

2. Translated by the International Labour Office, in its *The Labour and Trade Union Situation in Spain*, (Geneva, 1969), as "Trade Union Organization."

3. *Ibid.*, pp. 282-283. The head of the Organización is appointed by Franco. In turn the head appoints, directly or indirectly, the remaining officials of the parent organization of the sindicatos, who constitute the political elements of organization. Their principal task is to provide political direction to the sindicatos, ensuring that purely economic considerations are subordinated to political needs. The large technical and administrative staff working in the various departments of the Organización Sindical is under the direction of the political elements.

4. *Ibid.*, p. 207.

5. Personal interview with an economist in the Ministry of Labor, March 20, 1970.

6. See International Labour Office, *op. cit.*, p. 35, where the shortage of skilled workers is asserted.

7. At that time the official exchange rate was 60 pesetas per $1.00. In November 1967 the peseta was devalued to 70 to the $1.00.

8. *Hoja del Lunes* (Madrid), March 23, 1970.

9. As quoted in Tamames, *op. cit.*, pp. 189-190.

10. The Second Plan called for an annual review of the minimum wage, based upon the rise in the average productivity of the economy.

11. As quoted in *Iberian Sun* (Madrid), May 28, 1970.

12. Personal interview with an economist in the Ministry of Labor, March 20, 1970.

13. International Labour Office, *op. cit.*, pp. 52-53.

14. *Ibid.*, pp. 205-206.
15. OECD, *Economic Surveys: Spain,* January 1970, pp. 16-17.
16. *Ibid.*, p. 46 fn.
17. Comisaría del Plan de Desarrollo Económico y Social, *Hoja Informativa* 1/69, p. 67.
18. *Ya* (Madrid), May 28, 1970.
19. *Ya* (Madrid), August 9, 1970.
20. *Ya* (Madrid), January 23, 1971.
21. The basic reason for the low official rate is that only registered unemployment is considered. Unofficial estimates place unemployment at above 5 percent. In addition, during the past ten years about 8 percent of the labor force emigrated to other European countries, principally in search of employment. See chapter IV for a full discussion of the effects of migration on the labor force.
22. On this point, see footnote 49 in Chapter II.
23. Ministerio de Trabajo, Dirección General de Empleo, *Dinámica del empleo en 1964* (Madrid, February 1965), and *Dinámica del empleo en 1965* (Madrid 1966).
24. *Dinámica del empleo en 1965,* p. 14.
25. Instituto Nacional de Estadística, *Población activa en 1964* (Madrid, 1965).
26. These cities are Spanish territories on the coast of Morocco.
27. These statistics were derived by INE from its larger estimates of total labor force.
28. Fundación FOESSA, *op. cit.*, p. 1054.
29. The original table presented data for 47 occupational groups, based principally on the 2-digit code of the ILO's *International Standard Classification of Occupations.* These were combined by the author into more limited groups.
30. The table indicates 500,000 persons in the labor force worked zero hours, of whom only 135,000 were unemployed. If the 500,000 were excluded from the count of those who worked fewer than 30 hours, the percent would drop to about 3 percent.
31. Fundación FOESSA, *op. cit.*, p. 1056.
32. Information based on personal interviews with a number of persons in the Ministry of Labor.
33. Fundación FOESSA, *op. cit.*, p. 1056.
34. *Ibid.*, p. 1077.
35. ILO, *op. cit.*, pp. 35-36.
36. *Ibid.*, p. 36.
37. Ministerio de Trabajo, Instituto de Emigración, *Emigración española asistida* (Madrid 1969), *passim.*

Notes to Chapter IV

1. As indicated to the author in personal interviews with a number of the staff of the Planning Commissions.
2. International Bank for Reconstruction and Development, *The Economic Development of Spain* (The Johns Hopkins Press, Baltimore, 1963), pp. 345-346.
3. *Ibid.*, p. 344.
4. Ministerio de Trabajo, Dirección General de Empleo, *El empleo agrícola* (Madrid, 1967).
5. *Ibid.*, p. 4.
6. Unlike the labor force participation rates for the United States which uses the relevant population figure as the denominator (i.e., the population sixteen years and older), Spain uses a rate determined by dividing the labor force figure by the absolute total of the population.
7. Fundación FOESSA, *op. cit.*, p. 1078.
8. For a more complete discussion of the effects of migration, see end of this chapter.
9. International Labour Office, *The Labor and Trade Union Situation in Spain,* (Geneva, 1969), p. 35.
10. Comisaría del Plan de Desarrollo Económico y Social, *Factores humanos y sociales,* (Madrid, 1967), p. 33.

11. Ministerio de Trabajo, *Dinámica del empleo en 1964,* (Madrid, 1965), pp. 27-28.
12. *Ibid.*
13. Instituto Nacional de Estadística, *Anuario estadístico de España,* 1970, edición manual (Madrid, 1970), p. 53.
14. OECD, *Economic Surveys: Spain* (January 1971), p. 48.
15. If one went back to 1950, the net emigrants in that year represented 0.44 percent of the labor force.
16. Ministerio de Trabajo, *Dinámica del empleo en 1964,* (Madrid 1965), pp. 27-29.
17. Emigration in 1949 was 42,000; in 1948, 19,000; and in 1947, under 6,000. Earlier years showed emigration figures of less than 5,000 persons.
18. Instituto Nacional de Estadística, *Boletín mensual de estadística,* agosto-septiembre 1969, p. 25.
19. Comisaría del Plan de Desarrollo Económico y Social, Ponencia de Trabajo, *Unpublished report,* 1967, p. 21, states that without improvement in structure and mechanization, some 750,000 members of the labor force could be transferred to other economic sectors without diminishing total agricultural production.
20. Ramón Tamames, *Introducción a la económia española* (Madrid 1970), 5th edition, p. 343.
21. Based on personal interviews with persons in the government and in private industry.
22. Ministerio de Educación y Ciencia, *La educación en España; bases para una política educativa,* Madrid, 1969. This report is commonly referred to as "El Libro Blanco," the White Book.
23. Basic source is UNESCO, *Statistical Yearbook,* as quoted in Comisaría del Plan, *II Plan de desarrollo económica y social* (Madrid 1969), p. 92.
24. Fundación FOESSA, *op. cit.,* p. 953.
25. *Ibid.,* p. 955.
26. *Ibid.,* p. 964.
27. See Chapter V for a detailed analysis of Spain's educational and training system.
28. Comisaría del Plan, *Enseñanza y formación profesional,* p. 62.
29. José Luis Romero y Amando de Miguel, *El capital humano* (Madrid, 1969), p. 221.

Notes to Chapter V

1. Census data, quoted in Comisaría del Plan, *Enseñanza y formación profesional* (Anexo al Plan 1964-1967), p. 22.
2. Ministerio de Educacion y Cienca, *La educacion en Espana,* (Madrid, 1969), pp. 39-40.
3. Eight years of obligatory schooling, from six to fourteen years of age was not instituted until 1964.
4. Ministerio de Educación y Ciencia, *op. cit.,* p. 19.
5. Enseñanza libre, or free education, is a procedure whereby students may register for a program, take exams, and even receive a degree without attending classes.
6. The pre-university exam is given upon completion of a special one-year course after the higher baccalaureate, and is a prerequisite for all university programs. Failure of this exam precludes a student from university study.
7. Ministerio de Educación y Ciencia, *op. cit.,* p. 24.
8. *Ibid.,* p. 43.
9. This became law by Ley de Enseñanza Primaria, of December 21, 1965. It may be interesting to note that in a 1962 document prepared by the Ministry of Education in cooperation with UNESCO, the desire for obligatory schooling from 6 through 15 years of age was mentioned. See Romero y de Miguel, *op. cit.,* pp. 76-77.
10. Ministerio de Educación y Ciencia, *La educación en* España, (Madrid; 1967), p. 44-45.
11. *Ibid.,* p. 46.
12. The lower bachelor's degree 4-year program, considered as secondary education, is entered after the fourth year of primary school, and runs concurrently with the last four years of primary school. Also, it is possible to enter vocational training programs after the sixth year of primary school, but then the first two years of vocational training are con-

sidered "iniciación," or initiation, and they do not shorten the subsequent vocational training period.

13. Ministerio de Educación y Ciencia, *Datos y cifras de enseñanza en España*, 1969, pp. 41-71.

14. Ministerio de Educación y Ciencia, *La educación en España*, p. 61.

15. The persons taking and passing the exams may be from a larger universe than the entering class four years earlier. There are numbers of repeaters in each class, so the number (and percent) of those passing may include some students who entered the program prior to 1951-1952.

16. *Ibid.*, p. 63.

17. *Ibid.*, pp. 62-63.

18. Comisaría del Plan, *Enseñanza y formación profesional*, p. 42.

19. Ministerio de Educación, *La educación on España*, p. 71.

20. In 1967, about 9,500 completed the higher baccalaureate in letters and 35,200 in science. See INE, *Estadística de la enseñanza media en España, I*, Curso 1966-1967 (Madrid 1968), p. 54.

21. This technical baccalaureate program is a college-preparatory program for the study of architecture and engineering and should not be confused with various formal vocational training programs offered in the school system.

22. Comisaría del Plan, *Enseñanza y formación profesional*, pp. 46 and 49.

23. Ministerio de Educación, La educación en España, pp. 74-76.

24. There is a significant number of church and other private schools that are recognized or authorized to give vocational and technical courses and programs. These non-state centers meet certain standards with reference to content of programs and qualifications of teachers, and receive financial assistance from the state.

25. Architecture and engineering are not studied in what is called the university, but in these high-level technical institutes. These institutes are part of Spain's system of higher education, along with the universities.

26. Comisaría del Plan, *Enseñanza y formación profesional*, p. 51.

27. *Ibid.*

28. INE, *Datos y cifras de la enseñanza en España*, 1969, Tomo I, p. 119.

29. Comisaría del Plan, *Enseñanza y formación profesional*, p. 55.

30. INE, *Estadística de la enseñanza media en España*, II, Curso 1966-1967, pp. 120-121.

31. International Labour Office, *The Labor and Trade Union Situation in Spain*, pp. 159-160.

32. Information obtained through personal interviews.

33. Comisaría del Plan, *Enseñanza y formación profesional*, p. 62.

34. Statement by Director General of "Promoción Social" of Ministry of Labor on Tribuna TV, March 3, 1969.

35. Ministerio de Trabajo, *PPO Información*, No. 10, Junio, 1969, p. 14.

36. Comisaría del Plan, *Enseñanza y formación profesional*, pp. 62-63.

37. *Ibid.*, p. 63.

Notes to Chapter VI

1. Jaime Ballesteros, ed., *La Universidad* (Madrid: Editorial Ciencia Nueva, 1969), pp. 56-57.

2. *Ibid.*, pp. 57-58.

3. Pedro Lain Entralgo, *El problema de la universidad*, (Madrid: Editorial Cuadernos para el Diálogo, 1968), p. 93.

4. Ballesteros, *op. cit.*, p. 52.

5. Lain Entralgo, *op. cit.*, p. 103.

6. Ministerio de Educación y Ciencia, *La educación en España*, (Madrid, 1969), pp. 95-96.

7. *Ibid.*

8. *Ibid.*, p. 96.

9. In veterinary science Sevilla had two more students than Madrid, and in medicine, Barcelona had three more students than Madrid.

10. Antonio Tovar, *Universidad y educación de masas* (Barcelona: Ediciones Ariel, 1968), pp. 177-178.

11. *Ibid.*, p. 178.

12. Because of this movement to Madrid and Barcelona, the law specifies that vacancies in these two cities must be filled, alternately, by transfer and by an open national competition.

13. The basic laws, rules, and regulations of selecting and promoting professors have been developed over the years, but have been assembled in a single volume, Ministerio de Educación Nacional, Secretaría General Técnica, *Enseñanza Universitaria*, Cuadernos de Legislación 14 (Madrid 1965). Most information on this matter has been obtained from this volume.

14. Exceptions are made to this rule, and assistant professors continue in that position for years without ever attaining tenure or the welfare benefits that accrue to the agregado and the catedrático.

15. The professor can opt to work exclusively for the university (exclusiva dedicación), which means about forty hours per week. Under this arrangement he would receive about 10,000 pesetas per month additional ($145), but he would not be permitted outside work or outside income. There are not many professors who have selected this option.

16. Based upon discussions with a number of economics professors at the Autonomous University of Madrid.

17. Ministerio de Educación y Ciencia, *La educación en España*, (Madrid 1969), pp. 96-97.

18. The exception is that all courses of the freshman year must be passed within two years, before going on to the sophomore year. If a student does not pass all courses in two years, he may not continue his study in that faculty, although he may register elsewhere, without difficulty.

19. Ministerio de Educación y Ciencia, *op. cit.*, p. 90.

20. *Ibid.*

21. P. Laín Entralgo, *op. cit.*, pp. 21-22.

22. Ramón Bela, *Spanish Educational Reform-Three Views*, unpublished paper, June 1969, p. 9.

23. *Ibid.*, pp. 22-23.

24. As quoted in *Ya* (Madrid), November 15, 1969, p. 43.

25. Fundación FOESSA, *op. cit.*, Ch. 14, *passim.*

26. Based on personal interviews.

27. Ministerio de Educación y Ciencia, *La educación en España*, pp. 97-98.

28. This rather low ratio in the technological institutes may be the result of the significant number of instructors and teachers in laboratories, shops and "practical" classes.

29. Ministerio de Educación Nacional, *La educación y el desarrollo económico-social*, Madrid, junio 1962.

Notes to Chapter VII

1. *La Universidad* (Editorial Ciencia Nueva, S. L., Madrid, 1969), Colección "Los Complementarios," no. 16, p. 15.

2. Information obtained in personal interviews.

3. International Bank for Reconstruction and Development, *The Economic Development of Spain* (Baltimore: Johns Hopkins Press, 1963), p. 394.

4. OECD, *Technical Assistance and the Economic Development of Spain* (Paris, 1968), p. 22.

5. *Ibid.*, pp. 22-23.

6. *La educación y el desarrollo económico-social: objectivos de España para 1970* (Madrid, junio 1962). Report of a conference organized by Ministry of Education with co-operation of UNESCO, pp. 36-37.

7. Comisaría del Plan, Ponencia de Trabajo, Subponencia de Empleo, *Situación y pespectivos criterios* (Madrid, 1967, unpublished), p. 1. (Translated by author)

8. See annual report of Instituto Nacional de Estadistica, *Encuesta poblacion activa*, Table 5. (While these statics are discussed in official reports as employment data, they are actually labor force data, i.e., "activos." Since the official unemployment rate is well below 2 percent, the difference would not be too significant.)

9. *INE, Salarios, primer trimestre, año 1969* (Madrid, 1969), *passim*. Averages were computed by author.

10. "Necesidades y recursos de ingenieros civiles: Informe Matut," *Boletin informativo del instituto de ingenieros civiles de España*, Año XVII, julio-agosto 1969, Num. 99, pp. 21-103.

11. *Ibid.*, p. 40.

12. *Ya* (Madrid), November 28, 1969; and *Madrid*, May 2, 1970.

13. These comments are based upon personal interview. Little published criticism was made of the report.

14. Comisaría del Plan, *Ponencia de Trabajo del II Plan, 1968-71*. Anexo al capítula 1°, unpublished, p. 69.

15. In formulating both the first and second plans, the Planning Commission established many committees to write reports on special areas. One of the committees was a Committee on Labor (Ponencia de Trabajo).

16. Ministerio de Trabajo, *Dinámica del Empleo en 1964* (Madrid, 1965).

17. A draft of a 47-page document, entitled "Informe sobre planificación de empleo," was made available to the author. It was a basic document discussing a methodology that could be used in Spain to project the supply of and demand for labor.

18. Ministerio de Educación y Ciencia, *La educación en España: bases para una política educativa*, (Madrid, 1969).

19. José Luis Romero y Amando de Miguel, *op. cit.*, p. 74.

20. Untitled report, made available to the author by a member of the research team.

21. The official position taken by the Planning Commission was that the report would be published "shortly." However, some board members indicated that for various political reasons the report would never be published. The author did have an opportunity to read a copy of the draft, and it did contain some ideas on social justice which some politicos could find objectionable.

INDEX

Argentina, 7
Asociaciones Profesionales de Estudiantes, 99

Balcares, Province of, 62
Bank of Bilbao, 8, 13
Bank of Spain, 16
Barcelona, Autonomous University of, 89, 105
Barcelona, Province of, 38
Barcelona, University of, 89, 91, 95
Basque Area, 38
Belgium, 58, 118
Bilbao, Autonomous University of, 89, 105
Botella Llusia, José, 100

Cádiz, Province of, 51, 62
Carrero Blanco, Luis, 16
Ceuta, City of, 36
Chile, 7
Christian Democrats, 14, 16, 17, 124
Civil War, 11, 13, 16, 98, 124
Claustro Universitario, 88
Commission for Economic and Social Development Planning, *See* Planning Commission
Common Market, 4, 130
Communist Party, 17
Córdoba, Province of, 51
Cortes, 15, 16, 17
Council of Education, 91
Council of the Regency, 15
Curso de Orientación Universitaria, 107

Dinámica del empleo en 1965, 36
Dirección General de Empleo, 35, 118, 119

Economic Aid Agreement, 13
Escuelas Técnicas Superiores, 87

Faculty of Economics, 88, 89, 96, 98, 99, 100, 102, 105, 106
Faculty of Law, 89, 98
Faculty of Medicine, 89
Faculty of Pharmacy, 89, 98
Faculty of Philosophy and Letters, 89, 98
Faculty of Science, 88, 89
Faculty of Veterinary Science, 89, 98, 102
Falangists, 14, 15, 16, 17, 87, 120, 124
FOESSA, 51

Formación Professional Acelerado (FPA), 81
France, 7, 19, 54, 58, 64, 86, 89, 128
Franco, Francisco, 4, 5, 6, 7, 11, 14, 15, 16, 17, 34, 98, 124, 125, 130

General Law of Education and of Financing Education Reform, 107
Germany, 53, 58, 64, 118
Greece, 58
Gross National Product (GNP), 8, 19, 21

INE. *See* Instituto Nacional de Estadística
Informe Matut, 116
Instituto Nacional de Estadística (INE), 35, 36, 51, 118, 119, 120
Intensive Vocational Training Program (FIP), 82
Intergovernmental Committee for European Migration (ICEM), 56, 57
International Bank for Reconstruction and Development, 4, 8, 13 15, 45
International Labor Organization (ILO) 13, 42, 53, 119, 120
International Monetary Fund, 15, 18
Ireland, 7
Italy, 62, 64

Jaén, Province of, 51
Juan Carlos, Prince, 15
Junta de Facultad, 88
Junta de Gobierno, 88

Labor Board, 35
Labor Board of Planning Commission, 23
Labor Committee of Planning Commission, 114
Labor Panel, 122
La Laguna, Province of, 89
Law of Succession, 15
Ley de Formación Profesional, 81
Liberal Christian Democrats, 17
Liberal Monarchists, 17
Libro Blanco. *See* White Book
López Rodó, Laureano, 16, 21, 22

Madrid, 15
Madrid, Autonomous University of, 89, 100, 105, 106
Madrid, City of, 9, 27, 41, 51, 93, 99, 100, 113, 129

Madrid, Province of, 38, 62, 89
Madrid, University of, 89, 91, 99, 100
Málaga, Province of, 51
Marshall Plan, 13
Matut Archanco, José Luis, 116
Mediterranean Regional Project, 130
Melilla, City of, 36
Minister of Education and Science, 88
Ministry of Agriculture, 130
Ministry of Education, 58, 69, 74, 75, 76
    77, 88, 91, 92, 93, 94, 96, 99, 101, 104,
    105, 107, 111, 120, 121, 127, 130, 131
Ministry of Labor, 27, 35, 46, 55, 81, 82,
    111, 119, 120, 121, 127, 128
Murcia, Province of, 89
Mutual Defense Assistance Agreement, 13

National Institute of Industry (INI), 9, 12
National Institute of Statistics. See Insti-
    tuto Nacional de Estadística

Opus Dei, 4, 6, 14, 15, 16, 120, 124
Organizacion Sindical. See Sindicato Or-
    ganization
Organization for Economic Cooperation
    and Development (OECD), 9, 15, 130
Organización for European Economic
    Cooperation (OEEC) 14, 15, 18
Oviedo, University of, 96

Pact of Madrid, 1953, 13
Palencia, City of, 86
Parliament. See Cortes
Plan I, 21, 24, 35, 58, 130
Plan II, 23, 24, 121, 122, 130
Planning Commission, 19, 20, 34, 35, 45,
    47, 60, 111, 116, 118, 120, 121, 122, 127,
    128, 130, 131, 132
Program of Promotion of Workers Voca-
    tions (PPO), 82, 112, 121

Programa de Promoción Professional
    Obrera (PPO). See Program of Promo-
    tion of Workers Vocations
Pruebas de Madurez, 70
Pueblo, 17
Puerto Rico, 7

Romero Gomez, Emilio, 17

Salamanca, City of, 86
Salamanca, University of, 86
Servicio National de Encuadramiento y
    Colocación, 117
Sevilla, Province of, 51
Seville, University of, 96
Sindicato Español Universitario, 98
Sindicato Organization, 22, 26, 80, 81, 117,
    127
Socialist Party, 17
Somosaguas, 99
Stabilization Plan, 1959, 18
Sweden, 118
Switzerland, 7, 54, 58

Trade Union Collective Agreement Act, 16

UNESCO, 104
United Kingdom, 28, 97, 118
United Nations, 13
United States, 13, 16, 36, 49, 87, 91, 113,
    118
University at Somosagnas, 100

Valencia, University of, 95
Valladolid, University of, 95

White Book of Ministry of Education, 60,
    120, 121
Workers Committees, 17
World Bank. See International Bank for
    Reconstruction and Development